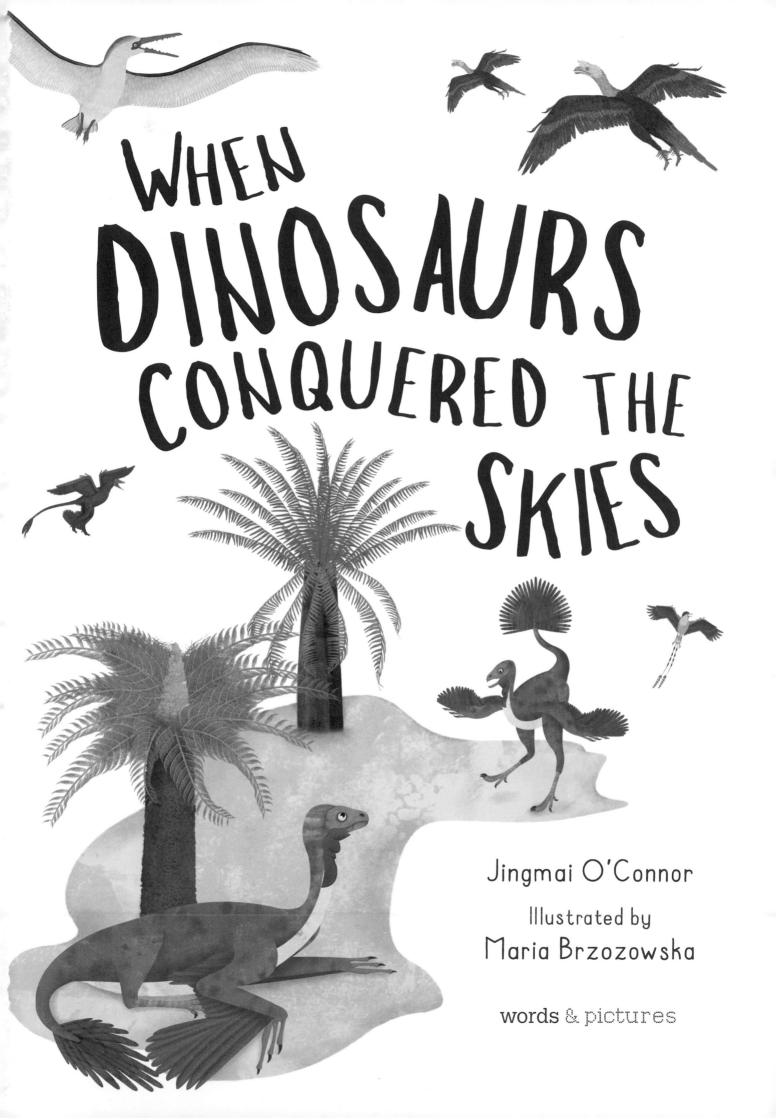

WHEN DINOSAURS CONQUERED THE SKIES

Jingmai O'Connor

Illustrated by
Maria Brzozowska

words & pictures

Brimming with creative inspiration, how-to projects, and useful information to enrich your everyday life, quarto.com is a favorite destination for those pursuing their interests and passions.

Inspiring | Educating | Creating | Entertaining

© 2022 Quarto Publishing Group USA Inc.
Text © 2022 Jingmai O'Connor
Illustrations © 2022 Maria Brzozowska

First published in 2022 by words & pictures,
an imprint of The Quarto Group.
100 Cummings Center,
Suite 265D Beverly,
MA 01915, USA.
T (978) 282-9590 F (978) 283-2742
www.quarto.com

Editor: Nancy Dickmann
Editorial Assistant: Alice Hobbs
Art Director: Susi Martin
Associate Publisher: Holly Willsher
Designer: Karen Hood

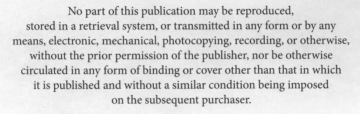

A CIP record for this book is available from the Library of Congress.

ISBN 978 0 7112 7515 7

Manufactured in Guangdong, China CC082022

9 8 7 6 5 4 3 2 1

FSC
www.fsc.org

MIX
Paper | Supporting
responsible forestry
FSC® C008047

"For my inspiring family."
JOC

"For Kosma."
MB

CONTENTS

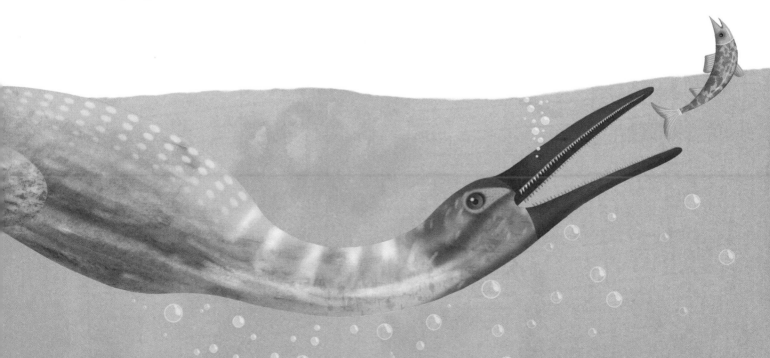

FASCINATING BIRDS

Birds are incredibly fascinating animals. They fly, they run, they swim, and they climb. They sing and they dance. They come in many different shapes and sizes and a rainbow of colors. And they are smart! Some are even capable of tool use and reading. But how did this wonderful group of animals first evolve? And what led to the incredible diversity we see today?

Birds everywhere

Did you know that there are approximately 10,000 species of living birds? That's more than twice the number of mammal species. Some scientists even estimate the number may be as high as 18,000! We are living in the Cenozoic era. Scientists often call it the "age of mammals"—but maybe it should be called the "age of birds" instead!

Birds are unique

Birds have one obvious difference from other animals: their feathers. But there are differences on the inside too: birds grow, breathe, and process food differently from other animals. In fact, birds are so different from other living animals that their origins have long been a mystery! In this book we will explore how birds became birds and how we humans finally figured it out.

Bird power!

Birds are capable of incredible physical feats, including flight. Flying takes more oxygen and more energy than running or swimming. Even so, bar-headed geese can fly over summits in the Himalayas that are more than 5 miles high. Many other birds, such as the bar-tailed godwit, migrate for thousands of miles, flying for up to 11 days without stopping. Feats like these are possible because of birds' unique bodies. Some features were inherited from dinosaurs, while other adaptations appeared during the evolution of the modern bird.

Birds are so strange it took us a long time to realize they are reptiles! The claws of the hoazin provide clues for biologists to follow

How science works

A lot of ideas that scientists had in the past have turned out to be wrong. This is because they didn't know all the pieces of the puzzle. But that's how science works! You make a hypothesis with the available information (like putting together the pieces of a puzzle), and when new information becomes available later on, sometimes it shows you were wrong and you have to correct yourself. Mistakes are part of the process. The famous scientist Isaac Newton once said, "If I have seen further it is by standing on the shoulders of giants." He meant that all scientific progress builds off the work done by the generations that came before us.

Living dinosaurs

When you look out the window and see a sparrow, you may not realize that you're looking at a little dinosaur! Come to think of it, many people reading this book have probably also eaten a dinosaur. We are taught that dinosaurs went extinct 66 million years ago, but this isn't completely true. One group survived and became incredibly successful—birds! We call this group Aves, which means *bird* in Latin. Scientists now realize that since dinosaurs are reptiles and birds are dinosaurs, birds are actually reptiles! When we talk about dinosaurs that are not birds, to be really accurate we should call them non-avian dinosaurs. However, to keep it simple, in this book when we say "dinosaurs" we mean non-avian dinosaurs, and when we say "birds" we mean avian dinosaurs.

FOSSILS AND GEOLOGICAL TIME

We know now that several groups of dinosaurs took to the skies and one group eventually ruled them. And the evidence that scientists used to piece the story together? Fossils! Fossils are rare and hard to find, but as they were collected over the past 160 years or so, we have slowly pieced together the story of where birds came from and how they became the creatures we know today.

Geologic timescale, 600 million years ago to the present

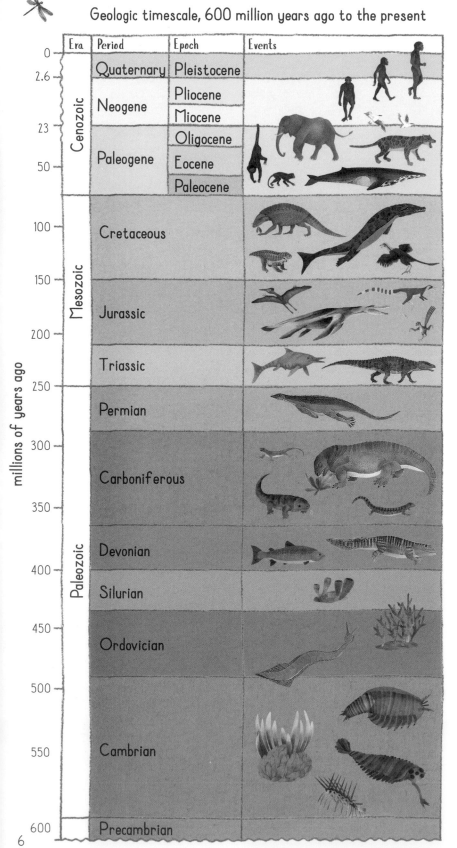

	Era	Period	Epoch	Events
0		Quaternary	Pleistocene	
2.6	Cenozoic	Neogene	Pliocene	
			Miocene	
23		Paleogene	Oligocene	
50			Eocene	
			Paleocene	
100	Mesozoic	Cretaceous		
150		Jurassic		
200				
		Triassic		
250		Permian		
300	Paleozoic	Carboniferous		
350				
		Devonian		
400		Silurian		
450		Ordovician		
500				
550		Cambrian		
600		Precambrian		

millions of years ago

History in a day

Earth formed approximately 4.65 billion years ago (BYA). It is really hard for people to comprehend timescales like this, but one way of thinking about it is to imagine that Earth's entire history fits into 24 hours. The Earth formed at midnight, at 6 a.m. the first microscopic life evolves, and land plants make their appearance just before 10 p.m. Birds first evolve at 11:10 p.m. and modern humans don't appear until the last second!

Geologic timescale

We divide Earth's long history into sections. The first 4 billion years are known as the Precambrian. The rest of Earth's history is divided into three eras: the Paleozoic (541–252 MYA), Mesozoic (252–66 MYA), and the Cenozoic (66 MYA–present). Each era is broken down into periods, then epochs, then ages. Our story begins in the Mesozoic, which is divided into the Triassic, Jurassic, and Cretaceous periods.

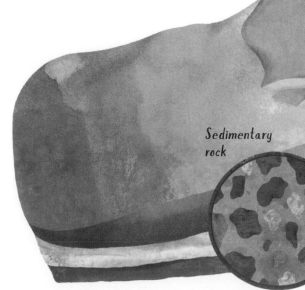

Sedimentary rock

6

Sedimentary rock

All rocks on Earth belong to one of three basic types: igneous, sedimentary, and metamorphic. Most fossils are found in sedimentary rocks. This type of rock forms when deposits of little pieces of old rock become cemented together to form new rock, like sandstone. And as this happens, sometimes the remains of organisms get trapped in the layers. These organisms tell us about what life was like when the rocks formed, and also help scientists estimate the age of the rock.

How we name fossils

When scientists find a new organism, living or extinct, they get to name it! The naming system we use starts with the species—the most exclusive group—and then moves up, with additional names that are made up of bigger groups of species. For example, the bird that we call the House sparrow has the scientific name *Passer domesticus*. *Passer* is the genus, which includes many other species of sparrows. The genus *Passer* is part of a larger family called Passeridae. Passeridae is part of a larger order called the Passeriformes. The Passeriformes is the largest order of living birds and includes 6,500 species—that's two-thirds of all known bird species.

WHAT ARE FOSSILS?

The remains of organisms that became trapped—and preserved—in sedimentary rocks are called fossils. Any life form, from tiny bacteria to the enormous *Tyrannosaurus rex*, can become a fossil, as long as it is buried in just the right type of conditions. Fossils can be body parts, or traces left behind by organisms when they were alive, such as fossil footprints. When an organism dies and gets buried, minerals in the water that seeps into the rock replace parts of the organism's body. Usually, only hard body parts such as shells or bones resist decay long enough to become fossils.

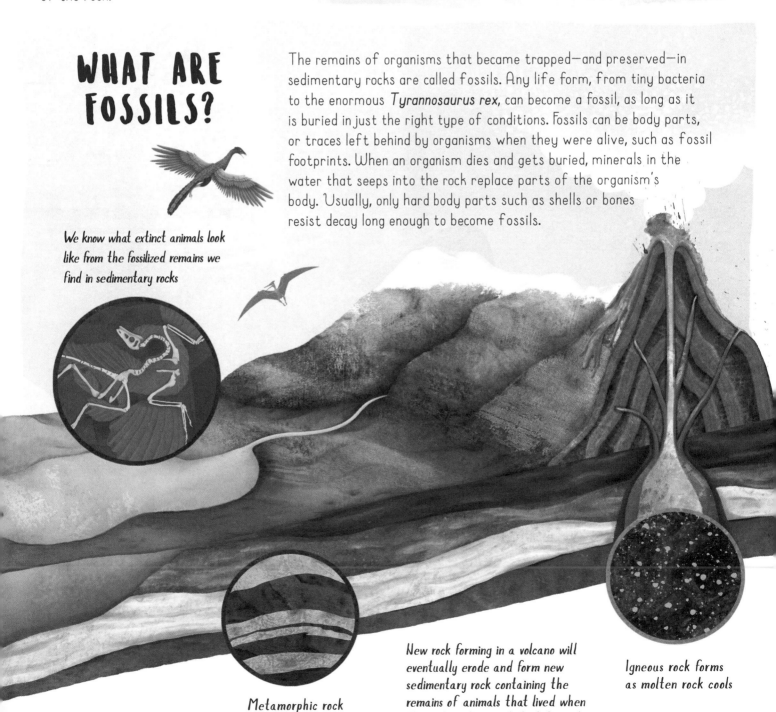

We know what extinct animals look like from the fossilized remains we find in sedimentary rocks

Metamorphic rock

New rock forming in a volcano will eventually erode and form new sedimentary rock containing the remains of animals that lived when the sedimentary rock first formed

Igneous rock forms as molten rock cools

FIRST FOSSILS: A DISCOVERY OF DINOSAURS

Humans probably collected fossils for thousands of years without really understanding what they were. Legends about dragons in Asia and Europe may have started when ancient peoples found fossils of big, extinct reptiles like dinosaurs.

Studying fossils

Xenophanes, a Greek philosopher living in the 6th century B.C., found seashells in rocks on dry land and realized that long ago, that land had been underwater. Over 1,500 years later, the Chinese philosopher Shen Kuo made similar observations. He was the first to use fossil evidence to understand that climates changed over time.

In the 16th century, Europeans began to classify nature and collected many fossils of prehistoric creatures, but they still didn't know what they really were. It was at this time that the term "fossil" was first coined. In Latin fossil simply means "thing that has been dug up."

The first dinosaur fossil

The first fossil dinosaur in the historical record of Western science was found in England and described by a man named Robert Plot in 1677. However, he did not know what he had found—the word "dinosaur" didn't even exist! The fossil was the bottom part of a femur, the upper bone in a leg. It was so big that Plot knew it could not have come from any animal alive in England at that time. First he thought it had belonged to a Roman war elephant, but later he thought it was the remnants of a legendary being like a giant or Titan. In fact, it was the femur of a dinosaur now called *Megalosaurus*.

Dinosaur finds in England

Between 1815 and 1824, Reverend William Buckland collected the fossilized remains of a large reptilian creature which he called *Megalosaurus* (Greek for "great lizard"). In 1825 Gideon Mantell described the remains of another large reptile. He thought the skeleton resembled the iguana and thus named this new species *Iguanodon*. In 1832 Mantell described another strange fossil which he named *Hylaeosaurus*. Today we know that all three of those reptiles were dinosaurs.

The amazing Mary Anning

Although Mary Anning (1799–1847) did not find dinosaurs, she deserves mention as the greatest fossil collector of the 19th century. Anning lived in Lyme Regis in southern England, where her family sold fossils to tourists. The rocks around Lyme Regis contain fossils of Jurassic sea creatures, such as ammonites (an extinct group of squid). Thanks to tirelesss searching, Anning, along with her brother, also found the remains of large extinct aquatic reptiles, including the first ichthyosaur and several plesiosaurs. She even found the first English remains of flying reptiles called pterosaurs. As a woman, Anning didn't get proper credit for her discoveries while alive, but we can celebrate her now!

A name at last!

England's scientific community took great interest in these strange discoveries. The paleontologist Sir Richard Owen recognized that *Iguanodon* and *Megalosaurus* shared features and were part of a group. In 1841 he named these reptiles "dinosaurs," (meaning "fearfully great lizards") because of their incredible size. Owen helped to establish the Natural History Museum in London to display the growing collection of fossilized remains.

THE DINOSAUR FAMILY TREE

Birds are dinosaurs, but not all dinosaurs are birds. The dinosaurs make up an incredibly diverse group, with species of all shapes and sizes. They have been around for approximately 242 million years and the bird branch of the family is still going strong! All dinosaurs share a common ancestor. From this unknown ancestor, which was small and walked on two legs, different families evolved in ways that helped them adapt to their environment. Dinosaurs that are closely related share a lot of features with each other.

TWO GROUPS

Early in the evolution of dinosaurs they split into two groups: Ornithischia (meaning bird-hipped in Greek) and Saurischia (meaning lizard-hipped). These names come from the orientation of the bones in the pelvis. Ornithischia includes all the armored dinosaurs, including stegosaurs, ceratopsians, ankylosaurs, and pachycephalosaurs. It also includes all the duck-billed dinosaurs. Almost all ornithischian dinosaurs were herbivores that fed on plants.

Surprisingly, birds belong to the lizard-hipped group! This is because they evolved from dinosaurs that originally had forward-facing hip bones. Saurischia includes the long-necked sauropods like *Diplodocus*. Some of the sauropods were enormous creatures, lumbering around on four thick legs, but the earliest species (called prosauropods) were small and walked on two legs.

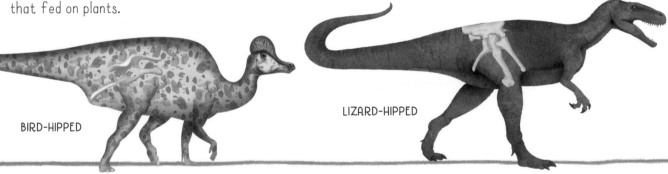

BIRD-HIPPED

LIZARD-HIPPED

AQUATIC DINOSAURS?

There are lots of extinct reptiles that we think of as dinosaurs, but which are actually not part of this group. Long-necked marine reptiles called plesiosaurs are not dinosaurs, and neither were the fierce mosasaurs or the dolphin-like ichthyosaurs. In fact, no dinosaur ever evolved to live entirely in the water. There are some dinosaurs, such as spinosaurs and penguins, that feed in water and are good swimmers, but they reproduce and sleep on land.

Plesiosaurs are not dinosaurs!

Theropods

Birds belong to a subgroup of Saurischia, the two-legged theropods. This group of dinosaurs also includes famous examples like *T. rex* and *Velociraptor*. All theropods are bipedal, meaning they walk on two legs. This meant that the forelimbs (arms) were free to evolve a new function, such as flight, in the case of birds. Most theropods were carnivorous.

Reptiles

Dinosaurs are reptiles, so that means birds are reptiles too! However, we don't usually think of birds when we use the word "reptile"—that's because until recently, we didn't know birds were reptiles! Scientists use another name, Sauropsida, for the group that consists of all reptiles including birds. There are many groups of reptiles. Dinosaurs and crocodiles are members of one group, while lizards and snakes form another.

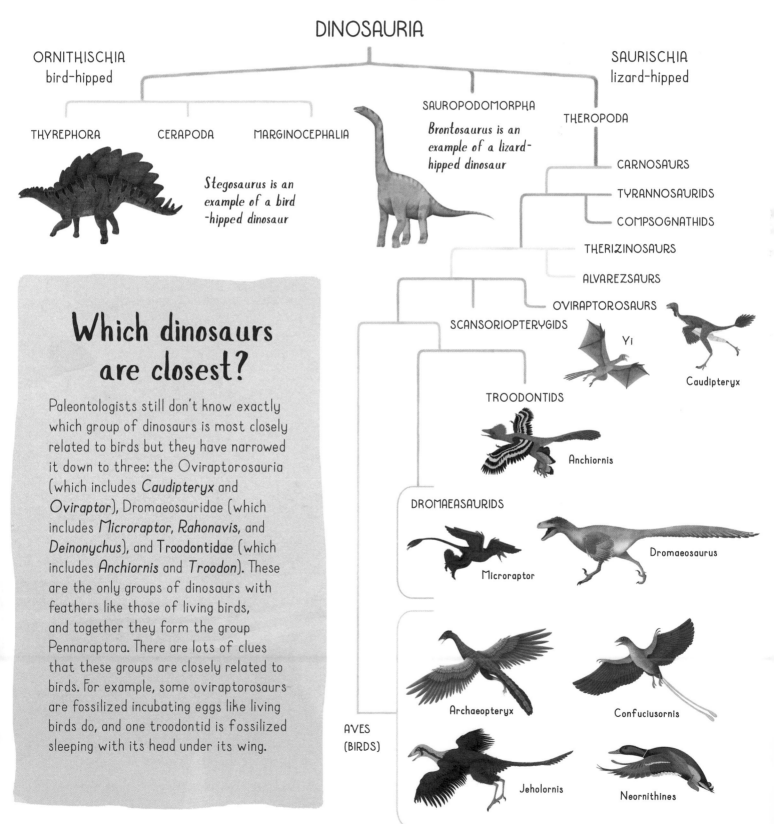

DINOSAURIA

ORNITHISCHIA
bird-hipped

SAURISCHIA
lizard-hipped

THYREPHORA   CERAPODA   MARGINOCEPHALIA

SAUROPODOMORPHA

Brontosaurus is an example of a lizard-hipped dinosaur

THEROPODA

CARNOSAURS

TYRANNOSAURIDS

COMPSOGNATHIDS

THERIZINOSAURS

ALVAREZSAURS

OVIRAPTOROSAURS

Stegosaurus is an example of a bird-hipped dinosaur

SCANSORIOPTERYGIDS

Yi

Caudipteryx

TROODONTIDS

Anchiornis

DROMAEOSAURIDS

Microraptor

Dromaeosaurus

Which dinosaurs are closest?

Paleontologists still don't know exactly which group of dinosaurs is most closely related to birds but they have narrowed it down to three: the Oviraptorosauria (which includes *Caudipteryx* and *Oviraptor*), Dromaeosauridae (which includes *Microraptor*, *Rahonavis*, and *Deinonychus*), and Troodontidae (which includes *Anchiornis* and *Troodon*). These are the only groups of dinosaurs with feathers like those of living birds, and together they form the group Pennaraptora. There are lots of clues that these groups are closely related to birds. For example, some oviraptorosaurs are fossilized incubating eggs like living birds do, and one troodontid is fossilized sleeping with its head under its wing.

AVES
(BIRDS)

Archaeopteryx

Confuciusornis

Jeholornis

Neornithines

YOUNG DARWIN

Fossils are hugely important to paleontologists because they record how living things have changed—or evolved—through time. And why is this change so important? In order to understand that, scientists first had to understand *how* it changes. Figuring this out was a true scientific breakthrough, and it's mostly thanks to the work of a naturalist named Charles Darwin. His brilliant insight into the process that produces evolutionary change was the result of his life's journey.

A young collector

Today most people live in cities. When growing up in the urban jungle there isn't much opportunity to learn about nature. Darwin, however, was born in 1809 and grew up in Shrewsbury, a market town in the English countryside. Back then there weren't any tablets or video games to play. His playground was the outdoors and even at an early age he was fascinated by nature. For fun he collected different kinds of beetles, moths, seashells, bird eggs, and minerals, and went birdwatching. Even at a young age Darwin was a budding naturalist.

Choosing a career

Darwin's father was a successful doctor and, like many parents, he wanted his son to follow in his footsteps. Darwin didn't have the stomach for surgery though, and he neglected his studies. Frustrated, his father then sent him to study to become a clergyman. However, Darwin's main interest was still the natural world. Although his grades were excellent, Darwin preferred being outdoors—riding horses and collecting beetles.

Geospiza
magnirostris

Geospiza fortis

Geospiza parvula

Certhidea olivacea

DARWIN'S FINCHES

On the Galápagos Islands, Darwin observed different species of finches. The shapes of their beaks varied a lot. Darwin originally identified these finches as representing many different groups, but after he returned to England he was corrected by an ornithologist (a scientist who studies birds). The different species were actually closely related but feeding on different things. The similarity between the Galápagos birds and those found on the South American continent helped Darwin to develop his ideas about evolution.

Cactus finch
on Galapagos

HMS *Beagle*

In 1831, one of Darwin's teachers recommended him for a position as a naturalist on HMS *Beagle*. This ship was planning a two-year voyage to chart the coast of South America. Darwin had to pay his own way, and the voyage ended up lasting almost five years, going completely around the world. All along the journey, Darwin studied the local geology and collected specimens of plants and animals. He also collected fossils in Patagonia. He took careful notes of everything he observed, and he sent many letters back to England telling of the things he saw and learned. These letters made him a scientific celebrity back home.

Ostrich

Exotic tastes

Darwin's interest in animals went beyond pure science—he was also interested in what they tasted like. While at Cambridge he formed the "Gourmet Club" (also known as the "Glutton Club"). Its purpose was to eat unusual animals. Some of the experiments were more successful than others—apparently brown owl tastes absolutely awful! Darwin continued this habit on HMS *Beagle*, eating all sorts of animals he encountered on his voyage, including ostrich, puma, and armadillo.

DARWIN'S BIG IDEA

In the early 19th century, as more and more fossils were collected, it had become clear to some scientists that animals had changed through time, and some had gone extinct. Before Darwin, several ideas were proposed to explain this change, but none were widely accepted.

Lamarckism

The first real theory of evolution came from Jean Baptiste Lamarck, a French naturalist whose theory was that organisms adapted to their local environment by using (or not using) particular features. For example, Lamarck thought that giraffes got their long necks by stretching to eat leaves in tall trees. Their necks would gradually lengthen and they would pass this length on to their offspring. But this is wrong, and it's not the only thing that Lamarck was wrong about—he also thought birds were related to turtles because they both have beaks.

THE RACE TO PUBLISH

Another naturalist, Alfred Russel Wallace, reached the same conclusions as Darwin. He wrote a letter to Darwin sharing his theory, making Darwin realize that it was time to publish his theory, or Wallace would beat him to it. The first published version of the theory consisted of Darwin's and Wallace's ideas presented together in 1858. Darwin finally published his book the following year, titled *On the origin of species by means of natural selection*. It was an immediate bestseller.

An idea takes shape

Darwin's observations during the journey of HMS *Beagle* led him to agree with other scientists that species change. Back home in England he read works by Thomas Malthus, who wrote that in human society limited resources result in competition for survival. Darwin also observed how animal breeders bring out traits in offspring through selective mating. All these things helped Darwin come up with the theory that made him famous. Darwin's idea was that in nature, individuals must compete to survive. Those that are better adapted than others are more likely to survive and reproduce. They pass their genetic traits to their offspring. In this way, species change over time, and some go extinct. He called this process natural selection.

The missing link

Darwin proposed the existence of extinct animals that would record evolutionary transformations. This means they would have features of both the group they evolved from and the group they eventually evolved *into*. No fossils of this kind of transitional organism were known at the time. Then, two years later, *Archaeopteryx* (AR-kee-OP-ter-ix) was discovered—a fossil bird with a long reptilian tail and a mouth full of teeth. Darwin did not seem very excited about this transitional fossil. This is because older fossil footprints of giant animals with three toes were thought to be evidence of giant birds that existed before *Archaeopteryx*. We now know these were formed by non-avian theropod dinosaurs.

Birds are dinosaurs?

Thomas Huxley was one of Darwin's strongest supporters in the debate surrounding natural selection. He studied the first *Archaeopteryx* skeleton as well as *Compsognathus*, a small dinosaur from the same deposits. Based on this comparison he suggested that birds were descended from small, bipedal, carnivorous dinosaurs. And he was right! However, the scientific community would not agree on this fact until over 100 years later.

Compsognathus

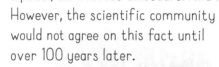

Microraptor

Microraptor
fossil

WHERE ARE THE FOSSIL BIRDS?

Birds have been around for at least 155 million years, but they are very rare in the fossil record. This makes it difficult to understand how they evolved. Fossils usually only tell us about the skeleton of an animal. We have to use clues in the shape of the bones to figure out the soft tissues like muscles and skin. However, in extraordinary circumstances, traces of soft tissues can be preserved—and what we can learn from them is truly amazing!

Small, thin, and hollow

Bird fossils are rare for three reasons: their bones are thin, often hollow, and small. The heavier a bird is, the more power it needs to flap its wings. Because of this, most birds are relatively small. The walls of their bones are thin compared to other vertebrates to help reduce body weight, which makes it easier to fly. Small, delicate, hollow bones are more likely to get destroyed by geological processes and are harder to find as fossils.

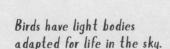

Birds have light bodies adapted for life in the sky.

Fossil lakes: windows to the past

The best place to find bird fossils is in rocks that were formed in lakes. Rivers bring a constant supply of sediment into the lake. That means, if a bird dies and falls into a lake, it will sink to the bottom and get buried by these river sediments. Lake bottoms are anoxic, meaning they have no oxygen—the perfect conditions for the bacteria that help the fossilization process. So why don't geologists just look for rocks formed by lakes? Well, lakes are relatively small, and in terms of geologic time, they don't last long. This means finding rocks formed by ancient lakes is not easy.

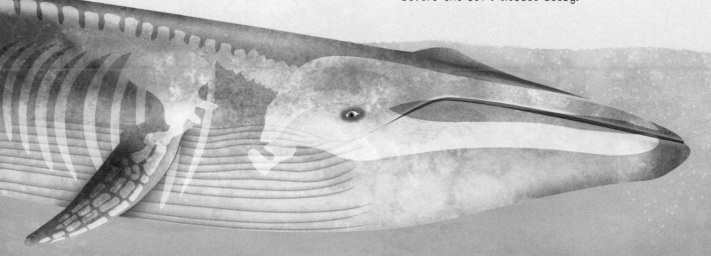

HOW WE FIND BIRD FOSSILS

Fossil collecting takes a lot of time and patience. Sometimes days (or even weeks) of work go by without finding any fossils. Most bird fossils come from ancient lakes or lagoons. The rocks that form in here are fine-grained and made up of thin layers. Paleontologists carefully remove rock, layer by layer, and inspect it for fossils. Bird fossils can also be found in other deposits like ancient sand dunes or rivers, but they are rare and often incomplete. Because they are rare, each bird fossil is important to our understanding of the evolution of birds and flight in dinosaurs.

1. A microraptor falls to the bottom of a lake.
2. Flesh and feathers decay to leave a skeleton.
3. Over time the microraptor fossilizes under layers of rock.
4. Millions of years later the fossil of the microraptor is found.

Soft tissues

While bones and other hard body parts like shells are most likely to fossilize, soft tissues like skin and muscles can do it too, although it doesn't happen very often. These rare soft tissue traces have contributed a lot to our understanding of the evolution of birds and flight in dinosaurs. However, the process that allows them to fossilize is still poorly understood. We know that it occurs best in water with hardly any oxygen. These anoxic conditions allow anaerobic bacteria to form biofilms that stabilize the soft tissues long enough for them to be replaced with minerals. The conditions also prevent scavengers from eating the carcass. Rapid burial is also important before the soft tissues decay.

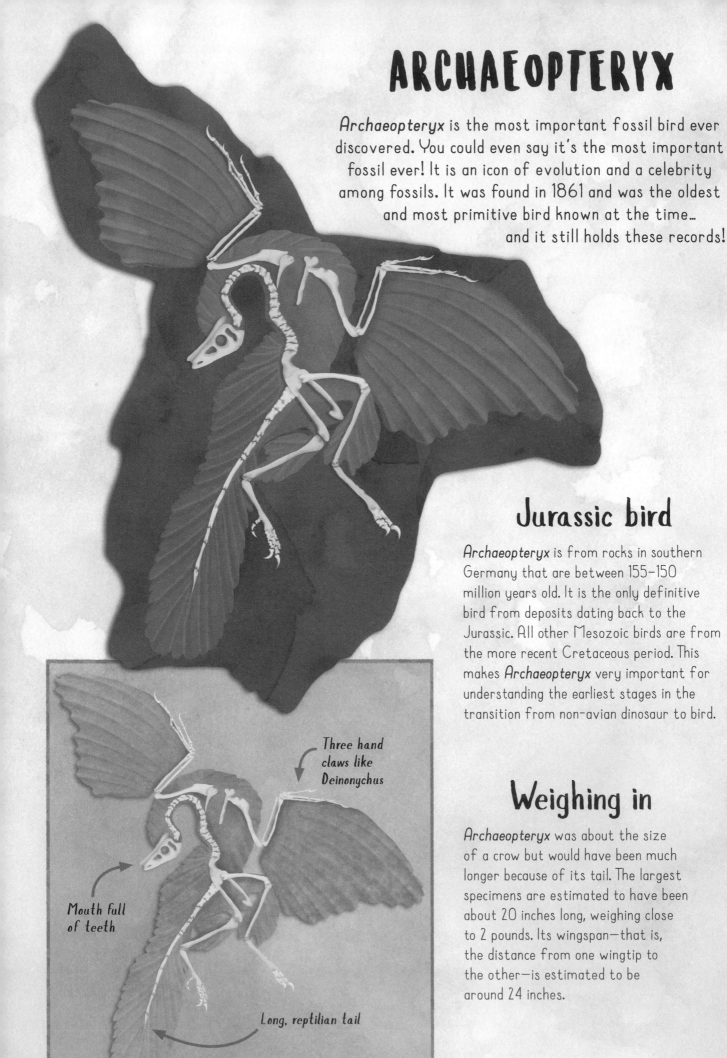

ARCHAEOPTERYX

Archaeopteryx is the most important fossil bird ever discovered. You could even say it's the most important fossil ever! It is an icon of evolution and a celebrity among fossils. It was found in 1861 and was the oldest and most primitive bird known at the time... and it still holds these records!

Jurassic bird

Archaeopteryx is from rocks in southern Germany that are between 155–150 million years old. It is the only definitive bird from deposits dating back to the Jurassic. All other Mesozoic birds are from the more recent Cretaceous period. This makes *Archaeopteryx* very important for understanding the earliest stages in the transition from non-avian dinosaur to bird.

Three hand claws like *Deinonychus*

Mouth full of teeth

Weighing in

Archaeopteryx was about the size of a crow but would have been much longer because of its tail. The largest specimens are estimated to have been about 20 inches long, weighing close to 2 pounds. Its wingspan—that is, the distance from one wingtip to the other—is estimated to be around 24 inches.

Long, reptilian tail

First feather

The first specimen ever found of this iconic creature was just a single feather! *Archaeopteryx* means ancient wing. In the 1860s, feathers were only known to occur in birds, so *Archaeopteryx* was easily identified as a bird. We now know that this feather was at least partially black and probably formed part of the wing.

A very rare bird

Even after 160 years, only 13 specimens of *Archaeopteryx* have ever been found: one feather and 12 skeletons. Each one is important, and scientists still don't agree on whether they represent a single species, or different ones. This is partly because they are not all the same size. The Haarlem specimen has even been suggested to be a non-avian dinosaur called *Ostromia*, but it is also the worst preserved specimen so it's hard to be sure.

Ancient lagoons

The limestone deposits in southern Germany where the *Archaeopteryx* fossils were found tell us that 155 million years ago, this region was part of a tropical archipelago. Between the islands were lagoons with limited connection to the open ocean. These lagoons were so salty that scavengers could not survive and the lower levels became almost anoxic. This created excellent conditions for animal remains to become fossilized—even their soft tissues, like *Archaeopteryx* feathers and jellyfish. Over 600 species have been described from these deposits, including 29 species of pterosaur.

THE MISSING LINK

Archaeopteryx provides the clues that link dinosaurs and birds. A century after Huxley studied the London *Archaeopteryx* fossil, an American paleontologist named John Ostrom discovered a new specimen of *Archaeopteryx* that had been misidentified as a pterosaur. He had also recently described *Deinonychus*, a theropod dinosaur found across the United States that belonged to the group Dromaeosauridae. Ostrom noticed many similarities between *Deinonychus* and *Archaeopteryx*. This lent support for Huxley's original hypothesis that birds are dinosaurs.

FEATHERED DINOSAURS FROM CHINA

One of the most important paleontological discoveries of the 20th century was made in northeastern China. It's called the Jehol Biota, made up of feathered dinosaurs and other organisms that lived alongside them between 135 and 120 MYA. These incredible fossils are preserved in rocks that formed in lakes. Volcanic eruptions often killed large numbers of animals at the same time, resulting in many fossils being preserved together on a single layer of rock. These rock layers are so rich in fossils that new species are constantly being discovered.

180 years of fossil finds

The first Jehol fossils finds were fish dating from the Mesozoic. They were found by French missionaries in the 1860s who didn't realize how old these fossils were. The first fossil reptiles were found in the 1930s and 1940s by Japanese scientists. They reported extinct species of lizards and turtles, as well as examples of a now extinct group of semi-aquatic reptiles. In the 1950s and 1960s, Chinese scientists conducted detailed studies of the geology and fish fossils. But there were more exciting discoveries to come...

Confuciusornis

An unexpected discovery

In 1992 a graduate student named Zhou Zhonghe was looking for fossil fish with his professor, the world famous fish specialist Dr. Chang Meemann. Zhou found something unexpected—a small bird! This was only the second Mesozoic bird ever found in China, and the first found in the Jehol deposits. Dr. Chang knew it was an important discovery and encouraged Zhou to study it. Dr. Zhou, who named the new species *Cathayornis*, is now one of the world's experts on fossil birds.

Cathayornis

A farmer's famous find

The region of northeastern China where the Jehol Biota is found is mainly farmland. Just a few years after Dr. Zhou's discovery a farmer was digging on his land when he found something strange. It was the nearly complete skeleton of a small dinosaur…but it preserved a halo of fuzzy-looking structures around the body that created a pattern of alternating light and dark stripes on the tail. This was *Sinosauropteryx*, the first feathered non-avian dinosaur ever discovered.

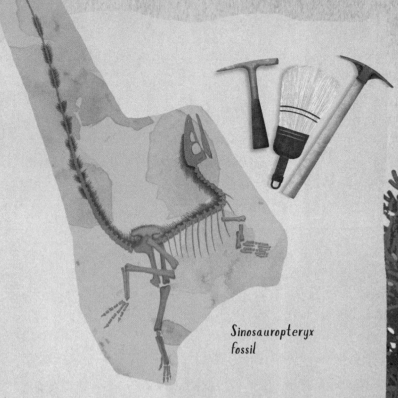

Sinosauropteryx fossil

Big digs

The discovery of feathered dinosaurs in China attracted an enormous amount of interest from both scientists and the public. Large teams of paleontologists conducted massive excavations, uncovering numerous specimens. However, even more Jehol fossils have been collected by farmers. Today, the Jehol is one of the most important fossil sites in the world and has produced over 40 species of non-avian dinosaurs, 70 genera of birds, and 30 species of pterosaurs. For some species, there are hundreds or even thousands of specimens.

HUXLEY WAS RIGHT!

The discovery of a feathered dinosaur was irrefutable evidence that birds are living dinosaurs. However, the *Sinosauropteryx* fossil merely had fuzzy structures…are they really feathers? After all, they look different than the feathers in *Archaeopteryx* and modern birds. But in 1998 even stronger evidence was found: a dinosaur named *Caudipteryx* that had modern-looking feathers on its arms, arranged like a wing. It was too small to be used for flight, but it indicates that feathers and feathers arranged into a wing shape are both features birds inherited from dinosaurs.

Caudipteryx

Sinosauropteryx

HOW FEATHERS EVOLVED

Feathers are one of the most distinctive features of living birds. They serve many important functions: they protect birds from UV rays, keep them warm, provide camouflage, allow them to fly, and are used to communicate within their species. Feathers today are very complex structures, but the very first feathers did not look this way. Instead, they were simple, unbranching structures. Fossils from China and elsewhere tell us how feathers evolved.

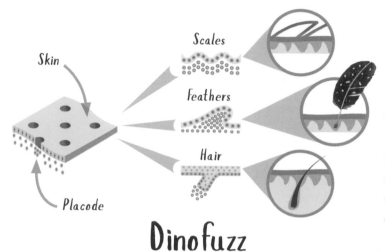

Skin

Scales

Feathers

Hair

Placode

It starts with a placode

Feathers are part of what we call the integument—the tough outer protective layer of tissue that includes skin, scales, feathers, and hair. Scales, feathers, and hair all evolved from a simple structure called a placode—a little bump or area of thickened skin. From the placode, each type of structure evolved in a different way.

Dinofuzz

The simplest type of feather found in dinosaurs is a single filament, kind of like a strand of hair. They aren't really like modern feathers so we call these structures proto-feathers or dinofuzz. They are found in many dinosaurs, including *Psittacosaurus* and *Yutyrannus*.

PSITTACOSAURUS

Pronounced: si-TAK-oh-SORE-us
Lived: 126–101 MYA (Early Cretaceous)
Size: 3.3–6.6 feet long

Psittacosaurus is a small relative of *Triceratops* that lived all across Asia. Its name means parrot-lizard (parrots belong to the order Psittaciformes) because it had a parrot-like hooked beak—but also teeth! One specimen was found that included soft tissue, revealing that *Psittacosaurus* was covered in scales and its tail had long, bristle-like proto-feathers sticking out.

Why did feathers evolve?

Feathers did not evolve to help birds fly. In fact, proto-feathers aren't even capable of forming a wing. Scientists aren't sure why they first evolved, but it may have been to help small dinosaurs regulate their body temperature, similar to mammal fur. Some scientists think that more complex feathers may have evolved to help animals attract mates or communicate with each other—like the extravagant tail in modern peacocks.

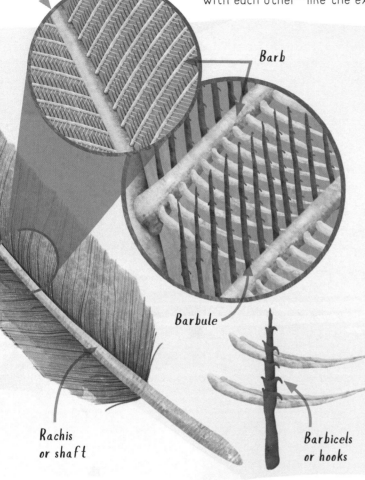

Rachis

Barb

Barbule

Rachis or shaft

Barbicels or hooks

Evolutionary progression from simple to complex feathers

PARTS OF A FEATHER

The spine of a modern feather is called the rachis, and barbs extend off it. Each barb has barbules extending off of it, and the barbules have barbicels—tiny hooks that interlock with those on the neighboring barbules. This type of feather is called a pennaceous feather. Scientists think that the primitive hair-like proto-feather is essentially a single barb. The next evolutionary step was a structure with several barbs joined at the base. This fused base formed the first rachis.

YUTYRANNUS

Pronounced: YOU-tie-RAN-us
Lived: 125 MYA (Early Cretaceous)
Size: 25–30 feet long

Yutyrannus is an early relative of *T. rex* that lived in the Jehol Biota. Although it was smaller than its famous relative, *Yutyrannus* had dinofuzz all over the body. Does this mean that *T. rex* also had dinofuzz? Some paleontologists think *T. rex* was covered in dinofuzz as a baby but lost most of its feathers as it got bigger. This is because really big animals have problems getting rid of body heat. They don't need dinofuzz or hair to keep themselves warm.

DINOSAURS IN COLOR

Not long ago, if you had told scientists they could discover the color of extinct dinosaurs, they might not have believed you. But it turns out that some of the structures responsible for color can fossilize. Studying these lets paleontologists understand what color some dinosaurs were.

Melanosomes

Melanosomes are tiny structures found in cells that contain pigments called melanins. Melanins in bird feathers help create the colors we see. Bird feathers are mostly made of keratin (the same material that fingernails are made of), with layers of melanosomes sandwiched inside. When paleontologists look at a fossil feather, it is actually only the tough melanosomes they are seeing. The keratin has rotted away.

Shape and color

In living birds melanosomes come in different shapes, and each shape corresponds to a specific color. Oval melanosomes are found in gray feathers, and sausage-shaped ones are found in black feathers. Reddish-brown feathers have round meatball-shaped melanosomes. The same range of shapes appears in fossil melanosomes, so we can work out the color of extinct animals.

EXAMPLES OF MELANOSOMES:

Gray

Black

Brown

Iridescent

SINOSAUROPTERYX

Pronounced: SIGH-no-sore-OP-ter-ix
Lived: 125 MYA (Early Cretaceous)
Size: 3.5 feet long

The fossil of *Sinosauropteryx*, a small theropod dinosaur related to *Compsognathus*, had a tail with alternating patches of feathers and no feathers. Scientists think that *Sinosauropteryx's* tail was striped because it is only the melanosomes of feathers that are preserved. The patches with no feathers preserved were white stripes, because white feathers do not have melanosomes.

STRUCTURAL COLORS

Some feather colors, including the beautiful blues, greens, and purples in a peacock, are caused by the actual structure of the feather. Microscopic pockets of air inside the feather change the way that light reflects from it, so sometimes we see a different color than the melanosome shape would indicate. These feathers can sometimes look iridescent, shimmering with rainbow colors. It is very rare for structural colors to fossilize, but there is one feather from 50 million years ago that still looks iridescent purple!

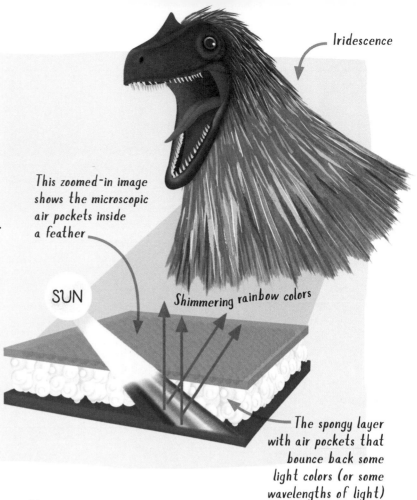

Iridescence

This zoomed-in image shows the microscopic air pockets inside a feather

SUN

Shimmering rainbow colors

The spongy layer with air pockets that bounce back some light colors (or some wavelengths of light)

CAIHONG

Pronounced: TSIGH-hong
Lived: 161 MYA (Late Jurassic)
Size: 16 inches long

Specimens of this troodontid dinosaur preserve spaces between the melanosomes—this probably shows that it had an iridescent structural color. That's why this species was named *Caihong*, which means "rainbow" in Mandarin. This dinosaur had crests on its face formed by bones called lacrimal bones. The very long tail feathers would have created a large frond-like structure.

Missing information

Melanosomes only give scientists part of the picture. Bird feathers also contain other pigments called carotenoids and porphyrins. Carotenoids mostly make yellow and orange colors, while porphyrins can make reds, pinks, browns, and even green. Scientists have not yet found examples of these types of pigments in fossils. Also, only small parts of a dinosaur specimen are tested for fossil melanosomes. So rather than knowing the color of a whole dinosaur, we actually only know the color of certain parts of the body. And animals are not always the same color all over— just think of a tiger or a peacock!

Austroraptor

Microraptor

Velociraptor

Dromaeosaurus

FIRST WINGS

Some theropod dinosaurs that did not fly had long pennaceous feathers on their arms—and in some species also on their legs! These feathers form a structure that looks very much like a wing, but these first dinosaur wings were not used for flight, so it might be better to call them proto-wings. Recent experiments are getting us closer to understanding how they became true wings.

Who has wings?

So far, in non-avian dinosaurs, pennaceous feathers are only found in the Pennaraptora—the group that includes the oviraptorosaurs, dromaeosaurids, and troodontids. These are also the only dinosaurs that preserve proto-wings. Proto-wings are present in all groups of pennaraptorans.

Wings before flight

In most Mesozoic pennaraptorans, the pennaceous feathers were only found on the arms, legs, and tail. The feathers overlap each other to form a large surface that resembles the wings of living birds. In most of these dinosaurs the arms were very short compared to the legs, and these proportions tell us that these dinosaurs could not fly. Proto-wings must have first evolved for some other purpose, and only later became adapted for flight.

Utahraptor

Deinonychus

Proto-wing mystery

So if they weren't for flying, what were proto-wings for? They may have been ornaments used to attract mates, but some paleontologists think that they might have had a secondary function. Proto-wings weren't big enough to get a dinosaur off the ground, but they could still produce a small amount of lift—enough to help them when running. In order to test this hypothesis, a group of engineers in China built a robotic set of *Caudipteryx* wings and attached them to baby ostriches. Then they measured the forces of the air on the wings with sensors as the ostriches ran around. The sensors showed that although *Caudipteryx* definitely could not fly, its proto-wings helped with running.

EVOLVING FOR A 3D WORLD

Flying is not easy! In addition to needing longer arms and pennaceous feathers, early birds needed bigger muscles to move the wings. They also needed modifications of the sensory organs to be able to move through a three-dimensional environment (the ground, where humans move around, is more of a 2D environment). It requires a bigger brain, excellent vision, and modifications of the inner ear that can detect motion and acceleration. Most of these adaptations appear in the dinosaurs most closely related to birds. Some have longer arms, while others show enlarged brains and an inner ear structure that resembles that of some birds today.

Enlarged brain

The beginning of flight

For a long time scientists argued about how avian flight evolved. One group thought that flight evolved from the ground up, as animals like *Caudipteryx*, whose wings were helpful while running, evolved bigger and bigger proto-wings. Eventually the surface area became large enough that the wings could lift the animal off the ground. The other group of scientists thought that the first flier was arboreal, meaning it lived in trees. It would have used its proto-wings to help while jumping from branches—first gliding and eventually flying. Experiments on baby chukars, birds related to chickens, support the ground up hypothesis.

Baby chukars

THE INCREDIBLE JEHOL BIOTA

Most of what we know about Cretaceous birds comes from the Jehol Biota.
This sequence of rocks formed between 135–120 MYA in northeastern China.
The fossils from these deposits are very special for two reasons. First, they
are really well preserved—there are numerous nearly whole skeletons, and many
also preserve rare traces like stomach contents and soft tissues.
Second, there are a lot of fossils! For some species, there are hundreds
or even thousands of specimens. This allows paleontologists to
understand these animals in incredible detail.

A spectacular diversity

The Jehol Biota includes a huge range of living things, such as non-avian
dinosaurs, ancestors of early mammals, and flowering plants. The birds of the
Jehol Biota are found in rocks that cover a 10-million-year timespan, though
there are more species in the younger rocks. The Jehol is
where paleontologists uncovered the first appearance
of many features we associate with birds today,
like short bony tails and toothless beaks.

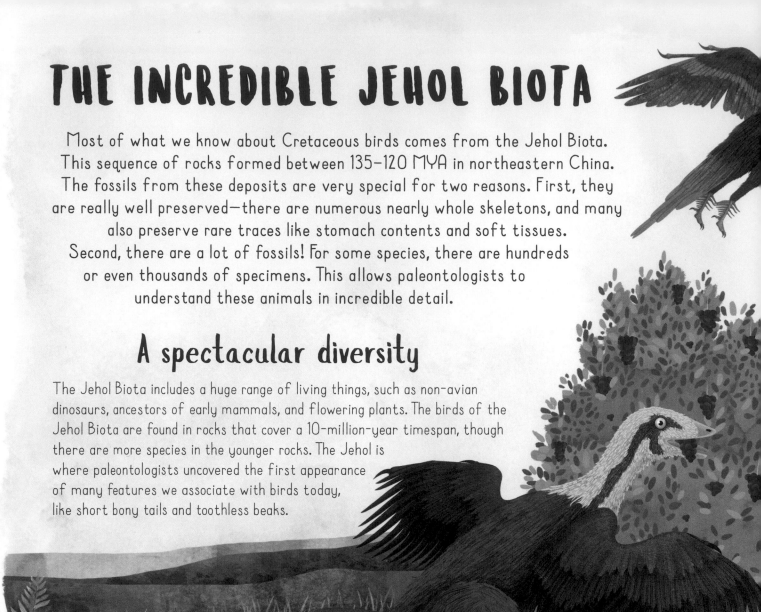

JEHOLORNIS

Pronounced: JEH-hole-OR-nis
Lived: 125–120 MYA (Early Cretaceous)
Size: 20–30 inches long; estimated 35–50 inch wingspan

Jeholornis was a relatively large bird with a long bony tail that helped it fly. Living birds help spread
the seeds of flowering plants (angiosperms) that produce fruits. Fruits did not evolve until the Late
Jurassic or Early Cretaceous, but many specimens of *Jeholornis* preserve plant traces in their stomach.
Scientists think these are the seeds of early fruit-bearing angiosperms. Birds like *Jeholornis* may have
helped spread angiosperm seed.

CONFUCIUSORNIS

Pronounced: con-FEW-shus-OR-niss
Lived: 125–120 MYA (Early Cretaceous)
Size: 12–18 inches long; estimated
20–26 inch wingspan

This bird had a big, sturdy skull with no teeth—the earliest known avian beak. It also had really big claws on its hands. Some specimens had long tail feathers that look kind of like badminton rackets, but the tails of other specimens were formed of short, wispy feathers. Scientists think that the long-tailed specimens were males. This is the earliest known evidence of males and females from the same species having different plumage. It's called sexual dimorphism and is common in birds today.

SAPEORNIS

Pronounced: SAY-pee-OR-nis
Lived: 125–120 MYA (Early Cretaceous)
Size: 12–16 inches long; estimated
30–40 inch wingspan

Sapeornis was about the same size as *Jeholornis* but it had longer wings and a short bony tail. This bird had a short face with big teeth in the upper jaw and tiny ones on the bottom. It also had tufts of feathers around its ankles and long tail feathers shaped like a fan. Just like living birds that eat seeds, *Sapeornis* had a crop that was low in the esophagus so that it sat on the chest, supporting the weight of the seeds. This bird swallowed stones to help grind up its food.

LONGIPTERYX

Pronounced: long-GIP-tair-ix
Lived: 120 MYA (Early Cretaceous)
Size: 9 inches long; estimated 18–20 inch wingspan

Longipteryx is an enantiornithine—you'll meet this group on the next spread. More than half of all species and specimens in the Jehol belong to this group. *Longipteryx* had long wings and an unusual skull. Its snout was much longer than all other enantiornithines and it had big, hooked teeth only at the tip of its jaws. The enamel of these teeth was more than 5 times thicker than that of other Cretaceous birds, but scientists aren't sure why.

RULERS OF THE CRETACEOUS SKIES

Enantiornithes is the main group of Cretaceous birds—in fact, half of all Mesozoic birds belong to this group! These birds flourished in the Cretaceous for 65 million years, and their fossils have been collected all over the world except Antarctica. However, they became extinct, along with the non-avian dinosaurs, when an asteroid crashed into Earth 66 MYA. If this group was so successful, why did they go extinct? It's one of the big mysteries of avian paleontology.

A controversial discovery

Almost 20 years before the first Jehol bird was found, a paleontologist named José Bonaparte found the huge bones of a new sauropod dinosaur called *Saltasaurus* in northern Argentina. When cleaning the bones he discovered that many strange little bones were mixed in with them. He gave the small bones to the British paleontologist Cyril Walker, who suggested that they belonged to a group of birds new to science.

Opposite birds

Dr. Walker named the group Enantiornithes, meaning "opposite birds," because the bones seemed to connect in ways that are opposite to what we see in living birds. But the bones were jumbled up and represented several different species, so some scientists thought that Dr. Walker was wrong, and the bones actually belonged to many different types of animals. Later discoveries showed that Dr. Walker was right about it being a completely new group of birds.

LIFE IN THE TREES

Although enantiornithines come in many shapes and sizes, the shape of the foot shows that nearly all of them lived in trees. In arboreal birds, the first toe points backwards and is very long. This allows it to work with the forward-facing toes to grip branches, similar to humans' opposable thumbs. The claws on the toes are all big and curved for extra grip. Birds that spend more time on the ground have a short first toe and short claws.

Super-super-precocial

Some birds, like sparrows and pigeons, are born helpless. They depend on their parents for food and protection, staying in the nest until they are fully grown. Other birds, like ducks and chickens, are born able to walk around and feed themselves. These birds are called precocial. One group of living birds called megapodes can actually fly right after hatching, so they are described as super-precocial. Enantiornithines were even *more* precocial—they were super-super-precocial! They could also fly right after hatching, but they flew a lot more. Fossils of baby enantiornithines show us that they hatched with their flight feathers fully formed and ready for flight.

Independent baby birds quickly take to the skies

ENANTIORNIS

Pronounced: ee-NAN-tee-OR-niss
Lived: 70 MYA (Late Cretaceous)
Size: estimated 15 inches long; estimated 50–55 inch wingspan

When Walker first named Enantiornithes he also named a species—*Enantiornis*. That makes *Enantiornis* the first official enantiornithine to be described. Not much is known about how this bird would have looked. Only a few wing bones are preserved, showing that it was a big bird with an impressive wingspan.

YUNGAVOLUCRIS

Pronounced: YOUNG-gav-oh-LOO-kris
Lived: 70 MYA (Late Cretaceous)
Size: estimated 10–15 inches; 40–55 inch wingspan

Yungavolucris is from the same deposits as *Enantiornis* and known only from one really weird-looking foot bone. It was short and stout and looks like it would have had a really big second toe. Paleontologists are not sure what this animal was doing with its strange-looking foot—it's tough to figure out extinct animals when the fossils are so incomplete.

OTHER FLYING DINOSAURS

Birds are not the only dinosaurs that could fly. We have recently learned that dinosaurs probably evolved flight at least four times! Several groups of dinosaurs had bird-like features, but now we know that these features don't necessarily mean that these dinosaurs were closely related to birds—they just mean that they were also flying.

Powered flight

Gliding

Types of flight

There are two different ways animals can fly: powered flight and gliding. In powered flight the wings flap to provide power. This type of flight is very versatile—you can take off from the ground, fly up and down, and fly in almost any type of condition, but it takes a lot of power. Gliding uses less energy, but it requires a high point to take off from, like a tree or a cliff. When gliding you lose height the farther you fly. Dinosaurs evolved both these forms of flight.

YI

Pronounced: ee
Lived: 163 MYA (Late Jurassic)
Size: estimated 12–14 inches long; 18-inch wingspan

Yi is a member of the oldest group of flying dinosaurs, the scansoriopterygids. This group had three fingers on each hand, with one finger much longer than the others. At first scientists thought this long finger was to help them catch food. Later, the discovery of *Yi* showed that the long finger probably supported a wing formed by skin, like those of pterosaurs or bats. Scansoriopterygids were probably gliders, but there is much we don't know about these little dinosaurs—only five specimens have ever been found.

MICRORAPTOR

Pronounced: MY-crow-RAP-tor
Lived: 120 MYA (Early Cretaceous)
Size: up to 30 inches long; 3.3-foot wingspan

The first specimen of *Microraptor* from the Jehol Biota was incomplete, but it was the smallest dinosaur known at the time. The second specimen was almost complete, with feathers all around the body. These feathers revealed something amazing: *Microraptor* had proper wings on its long arms…and on its legs too! These wings were big enough for flight. What's more, the feathers were asymmetrical. In living birds, this is a feature only found in flight feathers. These are clues that *Microraptor* was a four-winged flying dromaeosaurid dinosaur.

RAHONAVIS

Pronounced: RAH-hoe-NAY-vis
Lived: 70 MYA (Late Cretaceous)
Size: estimated 28 inches long; 50–55 inch wingspan

Rahonavis is a dinosaur from Late Cretaceous Madagascar. When scientists first discovered this dinosaur, they thought it was a bird (the "avis" part of its name means bird in Latin). Now most scientists think that it is actually a member of the dinosaur group Dromaeosauridae. The reason it looks so bird-like is because this dromaeosaurid evolved to fly. However, we don't know what kind of wings *Rahonavis* had because soft tissue does not preserve in the rocks in this area.

2 feathered wings

4 feathered wings

Wings made of skin

HOW DID DINOSAUR FLIGHT EVOLVE?

The idea that there was more than one group of flying dinosaurs is really new. Scientists are still trying to figure out how these flying dinosaurs are related to each other. Some scientists think that flight evolved only once, and all flying dinosaurs descended from this flying ancestor. However, we now know that some dinosaurs flew with two feathered wings, others flew with four, and some flew with wings made of skin. More and more scientists now think that flight evolved independently in each lineage of flying dinosaurs. This explains why their wings are so different.

33

CREATURES OF LAS HOYAS

In the Early Cretaceous, the land that is now part of central Spain was a vast wetland. The fossil beds of Las Hoyas, near the town of Cuenca, have produced many amazing fossils. They tell us about the animals that lived in this wetland, including many fossil birds. The first one, *Iberomesornis*, was discovered in 1980 by the Spanish paleontologist José Sanz. Later, other scientists realized that it was part of Cyril Walker's new group—the enantiornithines. In fact, all the birds that have been found at Las Hoyas are members of this group.

CONCORNIS

Pronounced: con-CORN-is
Lived: approximately 125 MYA (Early Cretaceous)
Size: estimated 6 inches long; 10–15 inch wingspan

Concornis is very unusual because it had two bones that are not present in other birds! The mystery bones lie where the coracoid (a bone in the shoulder) and sternum (breastbone) connect with each other. They may have been attached to the sternum by soft tissue. Scientists are not sure what these bones were for but in some living birds, like chickens, ribs become part of the sternum to form a similar structure.

EOALULAVIS

Pronounced: AY-oh-AH-loo-LAH-vis
Lived: approximately 125 MYA (Early Cretaceous)
Size: estimated 4–5 inches long; 10-inch wingspan

Eoalulavis preserves wing feathers that revealed an important feature called the alula—a little patch of feathers on the first finger that helps birds when they land or fly at slow speeds. The name *Eoalulavis* means "ancient alula." This adaptation means that enantiornithines were good fliers. *Eoalulavis* is also the only enantiornithine that preserves stomach contents. They show that it fed on small crustaceans.

BABY BIRDS FOR LUNCH?

One specimen from Las Hoyas consists of four baby birds all jumbled together. They are from three different species, and their bones show signs of being partially digested. This jumble of baby birds was probably a pellet, like the ones produced by owls. Owls eat their prey whole, and body parts like bones, which they can't digest, get packed together into a pellet and regurgitated. However, the animal that regurgitated this pellet is unknown. At least one troodontid (*Anchiornis*) is known to produce pellets, but no troodontids have yet been found at Las Hoyas.

SPINOLESTES

Pronounced: SPY-no-LESS-teez
Lived: approximately 125 MYA
(Early Cretaceous)
Size: 9.5 inches long

It's not just birds that have been found at Las Hoyas. One specimen of a mammal called *Spinolestes* is so well preserved that you can see the soft tissue of the ear and hairs! Traces of the lungs and liver were also preserved. This small animal had a mane around its neck and protospines on its back, sort of like a hedgehog.

CONCAVENATOR

Pronounced: CON-cuh-VEN-a-tor
Lived: approximately 125 MYA
(Early Cretaceous)
Size: 19–20 feet long

Perhaps the strangest of all the animals found at Las Hoyas is a theropod dinosaur named *Concavenator*. The vertebrae in its back have long growths that would have formed a pointed structure that looks like a shark fin! Some scientists think this may have helped *Concavenator* keep cool, but others think it might have been for display, to communicate with other *Concavenators*. *Concavenator* also has little knobs on one of its arm bones that suggest it would have had big proto-feathers sticking out.

BIRDS FROM CHANGMA

There is another place in China where many fossil birds have been found. These rocks, called the Xiagou Formation, are in northwestern China near a village called Changma—not far from the western end of the Great Wall. The rocks are about the same age as the youngest part of the Jehol Biota (120 MYA). Although only about 100 specimens have been found (compared to thousands from the Jehol deposits), these fossils are preserved uncrushed. This reveals some features that cannot be studied in Jehol specimens. Ten species of birds have been found so far.

If at first you don't succeed...

The first Mesozoic bird found in China was *Gansus*, named in 1984, but all that remained was its left foot. Then, 20 years later, a team of Chinese and American paleontologists revisited the area and found many new bird specimens. Almost all of them were more examples of *Gansus*, but some of them were more complete. However, no fully complete bird specimen has ever been found in Changma, which tells us that it took longer for these birds to become fossils.

Gansus fossils

GANSUS

Pronounced: GAHN-soos
Lived: approximately 120 MYA (Early Cretaceous)
Size: estimated 8–10 inches long;
15–20 inch wingspan

Gansus was a good flier, but it was adapted for feeding in water—it could use its feet to paddle around. The soft tissue of one specimen suggests that its toes were webbed. About 90 percent of all the specimens from Changma are *Gansus*, but scientists are not sure why. It could mean that this site was where *Gansus* gathered to lay their eggs, similar to the massive breeding colonies of seabirds we see today.

AVIMAIA

Pronounced: AY-vee-MY-uh
Lived: approximately 120 MYA
(Early Cretaceous)
Size: estimated 4–5 inches long;
10–15 inch wingspan

Avimaia means "mama-bird" because
the first specimen discovered has an
egg preserved inside its body, but the
egg is very strange—it has two layers
of eggshell. Each layer is unusually thin,
which may be why the egg got stuck
in the body and coated in shell a second
time. When a bird's egg becomes stuck
inside the body, it is called egg-binding.
Egg-binding is fatal in wild birds, so this
specimen of *Avimaia* may have been
killed by the egg stuck in its body.

FEITIANIUS

Pronounced: fay-TYEN-ee-us
Lived: approximately 120 MYA
(Early Cretaceous)
Size: estimated 4–5 inches long;
10–15 inch wingspan

The egg found inside *Avimaia* showed that
it was a female. The first specimen of a
bird called *Feitianius* had a different clue:
an extravagant tail made of feathers in
different shapes and sizes. A few species
of living birds have super-fancy tails
like this, and in these species the fancy
plumage is only present in the male. This is
why scientists think that the specimen of
Feitianius is probably a male.

QILIANIA

Pronounced: chee-LEN-ee-uh
Lived: approximately 120 MYA (Early Cretaceous)
Size: estimated 4–5 inches long; 10–15 inch wingspan

This enantiornithine is named after the beautiful Qilian mountains
that tower over the Xiagou Formation. (The species name of this fossil
bird, *Qiliania graffini*, honors Greg Graffin, a rock star who is also a
paleontologist!) Two specimens of *Qiliania* are known, and although the bones
are beautifully preserved, there is no soft tissue.

WHAT DID THE FIRST BIRDS EAT?

Powered flight requires a lot of energy, so birds need to eat a lot. The avian digestive system helps birds get the most energy possible from the food they eat. But this special digestive system did not evolve all at once. Some features were inherited from birds' closest non-avian dinosaur relatives. Other features evolved in the Cretaceous as birds became more and more adapted for powered flight.

Super-efficient

Compared to mammals, the digestive system of birds is shorter and lighter, which helps keep birds' bodies from being too heavy to fly. Birds have an extension of the esophagus that forms a pouch called the crop, where they store excess food. Birds can also move food from the intestines back into the stomach, then into the intestines again. By using the same part of the intestines over and over, they can get the most nutrients out of their food.

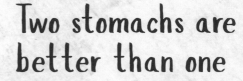

Esophagus

Lungs

Gizzard

Crop

Front stomach

Intestines

Two stomachs are better than one

Birds have two stomachs, each with a different function. The front stomach produces digestive juices and the back stomach (called the gizzard) breaks down food. Birds that eat hard foods like plant seeds swallow stones that help to smash up the food in the gizzard. Birds inherited this two-part stomach from non-avian dinosaurs. Some dinosaurs, including *Psittacosaurus* and *Caudipteryx*, preserve clusters of stones called gastroliths where the stomach should be—this shows they also had a grinding gizzard.

Owl pellets

PELLETS

Most birds eat their prey whole, but they can't digest all of it quickly. Unwanted body parts like bones, hair, and feathers are just additional weight that would make it harder to fly. So these birds regurgitate all the unwanted parts in a ball called a pellet. It's like barfing, but on purpose! This is another feature that birds may have inherited from non-avian dinosaurs.

ANCHIORNIS

Pronounced: AN-key-OR-nis
Lived: 163 MYA (Late Jurassic)
Size: 12–18 inches long

One specimen of the troodontid dinosaur *Anchiornis* preserves a ball of lizard bones in its throat. Scientists think this was a pellet that was about to be cast (regurgitated) when the animal died. Fossilized melanosomes tell scientists *Anchiornis* was dark gray, but the crown feathers were reddish, and there were reddish spots on the face. The leg feathers were white with black spots at the end.

YANORNIS

Pronounced: YANN-OR-nis
Lived: 125–120 MYA (Early Cretaceous)
Size: 12–13 inches long with estimated 30–32 inch wingspan

Many specimens of *Yanornis* preserve fish inside the body, including whole fish found in the crop. This tells us that even though *Yanornis* had lots of teeth, it swallowed fish whole. Mashed-up fish bones are found in the stomach and there are fish-bone pellets in the esophagus. Like many living fish-eating birds, *Yanornis* cast pellets containing the hard-to-digest bones and scales.

Prehistoric bird—teeth

Modern bird—no teeth

Teeth vs beak

No living birds have teeth—the bones that form the mouth are covered in a keratin sheath that forms a beak. Teeth were lost during the evolution of birds at least five times (probably more), and it also happened during the evolution of some non-avian theropod dinosaurs. Birds don't use teeth to chew, but they probably helped carnivorous birds catch prey. Scientists are not sure why herbivorous birds and dinosaurs lost their teeth. It might be because they didn't use them, so they became lost.

BABY BIRDS

The way birds reproduce and raise their babies is unique. They lay only an egg a day, every day, until their clutch is complete. They also use their body heat to incubate (keep warm) their eggs. Birds with babies that are born naked and helpless feed them every day until they are fully grown. Birds inherited some of these reproductive traits from their closest dinosaur ancestors, while others evolved during the Cretaceous.

Dinosaur babies

Most non-avian dinosaurs did not take care of their young. They probably dug holes and laid their entire clutch of eggs all at once, like turtles and crocodiles. Burying the clutch with rotting vegetation kept the eggs warm. The dinosaurs probably protected their nests, and when the babies hatched, they were able to feed themselves.

ONE OVARY OR TWO?

Most vertebrates that live on land have two functional ovaries—the female organs that contain egg cells. This includes dinosaurs. However, most birds only have one—the left. The right is vestigial, meaning only a small remnant of it remains. Several extraordinary bird specimens from the Jehol show that Early Cretaceous birds already had only one ovary. The loss of the right ovary must have occurred somewhere between oviraptorosaurs, which laid eggs in pairs, and the first birds. Scientists think that flight was the reason the right ovary was lost. Trying to take off with one egg inside you is difficult—two is worse!

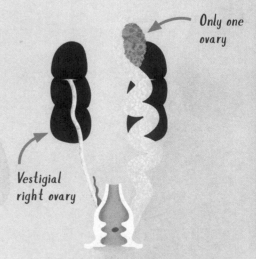

Only one ovary

Vestigial right ovary

BIRDS REPRODUCTIVE SYSTEM

Good parents

There is evidence that some dinosaurs, including pennaraptorans, took care of their young. Beautiful fossils preserve oviraptorosaur dinosaurs sitting inside a ring of eggs with their arms spread out protectively. Some eggs even include developing embryos, suggesting that the eggs were incubated with body heat, like those of living birds. Early birds probably incubated their eggs too—one fossil site in Romania preserves embryonic enantiornithine bones together with the bones of adults.

chalazae

embryo

An egg-cellent innovation

The eggs of living birds have two membranes called chalazae. They extend from either end of the egg, holding the embryo in place. This allows birds to move and rotate their eggs so the embryo grows faster. Crocodilian eggs do not have chalazae, so if you rotate a crocodile egg, the embryo will die. Some enantiornithine nests show that enantiornithines laid their eggs in mud and probably did not move them. These primitive birds likely did not have chalazae—a feature that may have only evolved in modern birds, helping them to survive the end Cretaceous mass extinction.

Oviraptorosaur (pennaraptoran) egg

HARD AND COLORFUL

Living crocodilians and birds have hard-shelled eggs, so scientists thought dinosaurs must have had hard eggs too. But fossil eggs have only been found for three groups of dinosaurs: hadrosaurids (duckbills), sauropods (long necks), and theropods (including birds). Each group's eggshells look very different from the others. We now know this is because the hard eggshell evolved three different times. Most dinosaurs laid soft-shelled eggs instead, like snakes and turtles do, and those shells don't preserve.

Today, only birds have eggs that are colored, though not all bird eggs are colorful. Fossilized pigments show that only pennaraptorans had colored eggs. This is related to a change in nest structure: pennaraptorans, like birds today, built open nests rather than burying the eggs.

Trodoontid (theropod) egg

Sauropod egg

Hadrosaurid egg

Oviraptorosaur (pennaraptoran) egg

A TALE OF TAILS

Living birds have tail feathers that come in all shapes and sizes. Tails *can* help birds fly better, but they don't *have* to. Some birds evolved aerodynamic tail shapes, while others evolved extravagant ornamental tails, like that of a peacock. Mesozoic birds were the same—some had tails that helped them fly and some had tails that helped them attract mates...and some had both!

Jeholornis

Reptilian tails

The first birds' tails were totally unlike those of birds today. They were long and formed by many bones, like those of non-avian dinosaurs and other reptiles. We only know of two birds (*Archaeopteryx* and *Jeholornis*) with tails like this, but there probably were others—we just haven't found them yet! *Archaeopteryx* had 21–23 tail vertebrae, while *Jeholornis* had 27.

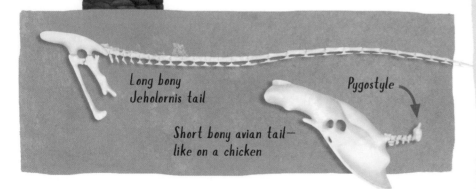

Long bony
Jeholornis tail

Short bony avian tail—
like on a chicken

Pygostyle

ALL SHAPES AND SIZES

Even back in the Cretaceous, birds had lots of different tail shapes. *Confuciusornis* and most enantiornithines had long ornamental tail feathers that were only present in males. *Sapeornis* and ornithuromorph birds had long, fan-shaped tails. The fan is used during slow flight, such as landing, but kept folded when flying fast so that it doesn't create drag.

Confuciusornis

Sapeornis

Evolution of the pygostyle

Almost all birds have a short bony tail, with very few vertebrae. The vertebrae at the end of the tail became fused, forming a pygostyle. There are no bird fossils that record the transition from a long to a short tail. Genes show that it was probably an abrupt transition—one mutation can make an animal with a long tail have a short tail, and this is probably what happened in bird evolution.

Sexual selection

Darwin recognized that some features do not seem to help an animal survive. He hypothesized that these features evolved through "sexual selection." They help animals to attract mates so that they have more offspring to pass on their genes. But ornaments take energy to grow and make it harder to move around. Birds that need to fly a lot and cannot hide, like seabirds, do not have ornamental tails. Birds in tropical forests often do, because they fly less.

Seabird

Tropical bird

ARCHAEORHYNCHUS

Pronounced: AR-key-oh-RIN-kus
Lived: 125–120 MYA
Size: 7 inches long; estimated 20-inch wingspan

This bird had a pin-tail consisting of a fan of feathers with two long, narrow ornamental feathers called pins. This tail shape helps with flight and also attracts mates, so it evolved many times in both modern birds and Cretaceous birds. Pins have very little cost because their narrow shape produces little drag.

PARAPROTOPTERYX

Pronounced: PAIR-uh-pro-TOP-ter-ix
Lived: 125 MYA
Size: estimated 4–5 inches long; 10–12 inch wingspan

In most enantiornithines, the ornamental feathers are called racket-plumes because they are shaped like badminton rackets. The narrow part of the feather reduces drag. Racket-plumes have evolved many times, but the ones in Cretaceous birds were different from those in living birds. The rachis was very wide, so we call them rachis-dominated feathers, but they are now extinct. Most enantiornithines had only two racket-plumes, but *Paraprotopteryx* had four.

THE EVOLUTION OF FLIGHT

Archaeopteryx could fly, but its body was totally different from that of living birds. Its skeleton lacked most of the features associated with flight, and it probably wasn't very good at flying—at least, not compared to modern birds. During the Cretaceous, through the process of natural selection, the skeletons and soft tissues of birds became better adapted for flight.

The power of patagia

The feathers of a bird's wing are supplemented by flaps of skin called patagia. Modern birds have three different patagia, and fossils tell us the order in which they evolved. The postpatagium, which extends along the back of the hand, evolved first. Next came the propatagium, connecting the shoulder to the wrist. Finally, an alular patagium evolved, extending from the first finger of the wing to the second, where the main flight feathers attach.

Alular patagium

Propatagium

No claws

No teeth

Three claws

Teeth

Postpatagium

No sternum

ARCHAEOPTERYX

Short tail

Long tail

Large sternum

MODERN BIRD

Flight muscles

Two muscles are important for flight: the pectoralis and supracoracoideus. The pectoralis is responsible for the downward part of wing flapping. The smaller supracoracoideus powers the upstroke, which takes less muscle power. Both muscles attach to a bone called the sternum. As the sternum evolved to be bigger, it provided more surface area for the attachment of larger flight muscles. Birds also evolved a keel that sticks down from the sternum, giving even more area for muscle attachment. The earliest enantiornithines had very small keels, but by the Late Cretaceous they were bigger—so Late Cretaceous enantiornithines had bigger flight muscles and were better fliers.

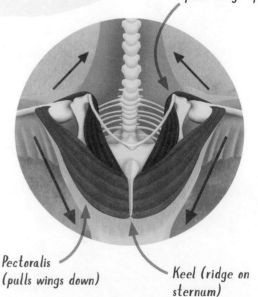

Supracoracoideus (pulls wings up)

Pectoralis (pulls wings down)

Keel (ridge on sternum)

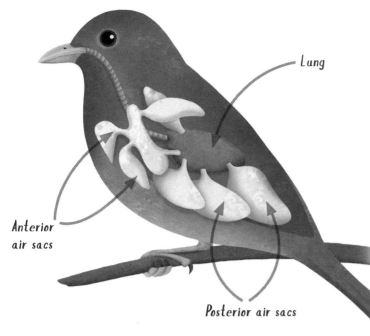

It's all in the lungs

Mammals breathe air into the lungs, then breathe it out. This is not very efficient, because oxygen only enters the lungs half of the time. In birds, the air goes in one direction through the lungs—as new air is brought in one end, old air is expelled out the other. Birds have air sacs that contract to move air through the respiratory system. This efficient system allows birds to breathe at high elevations, where there is less oxygen. Air sacs even fill the hollow spaces in some bones, making the skeleton even lighter.

Lung

Anterior air sacs

Posterior air sacs

BIRD BRAINS

Although people use "birdbrain" as an insult, birds are actually very smart! They can do lots of things that scientists used to think were unique to humans and chimpanzees. For example, birds can recognize themselves in the mirror and learn complex sounds by hearing them. They communicate, use tools, and remember where they hid food. They can follow a human's gaze and even know if they are being watched! Their brains are small, but more efficient than ours. A small brain weighs less, which is better for flight. The brains of Mesozoic birds were smaller than those of living birds—brain size increased after the end of the Cretaceous.

I'm a pretty bird!

A bird's eye view

Birds have really good vision, which is necessary for flying safely. They have large eyes in proportion to their body but can't move their eyes much in their sockets—they move their heads instead. Most birds can see UV light, so the world would look very different through a bird's eye view! Scientists think that some birds can even "see" Earth's magnetic field, using it to navigate. Birds inherited their excellent vision from theropod dinosaurs.

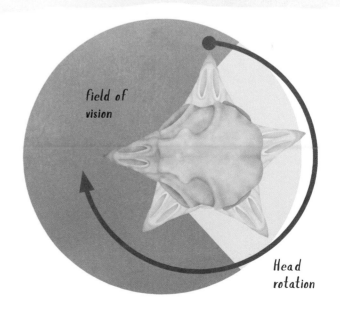

field of vision

Head rotation

BIRDS GROW FAST!

One special feature of modern birds is that they grow very quickly—almost all species reach adult size by their first birthday, and some do it in just a few weeks! Dinosaurs, on the other hand, took many years to reach adult size. Growing fast requires a lot of energy and is possible because birds are warm blooded. But how did birds evolve this special type of rapid growth? The clues lie in the fossilized bones of extinct dinosaurs and early birds.

Paleohistology

Paleontologists know how dinosaurs and early birds grew by looking at the structure of their bone tissue under a microscope. The study of tissue at a microscopic level is called histology. And when those tissues are ancient, it's called paleohistology. Paleohistologists take pieces of fossil bone and cut them very thin—about the width of a human hair. Then they are studied under a microscope. Magnifying the bone by about 40 times means that many different details can be studied.

DINOSAUR FEMUR BONE

Hollow medullary cavity

Rings that show how many years the dinosaur lived

Fast growth

Slow growth

The distance between the rings shows how fast they grew

x40 ZOOM

Growth rings

Although the cells that live in bone (called osteocytes) are not fossilized, through a microscope we can see the little chambers in which each one would have lived. Dinosaurs don't grow continuously all year round. When food is more limited during the winter, they stop growing and a line forms in their bone tissue—just like the rings in a tree trunk. By counting the lines, paleontologists can estimate how old a dinosaur was when it died. And by measuring the distance between each line, they can tell how fast the dinosaur grew each year.

GROWTH IN MESOZOIC BIRDS

A South African paleohistologist named Anusuya Chinsamy-Turan was the first person to study the bone tissue of Mesozoic birds. The enantiornithine bones she cut showed that these birds grew very slowly for many years. As more and more enantiornithine bones were studied, it became clear that enantiornithines grew in different ways, and some grew faster than others. However, all of them were like dinosaurs because they took several years to grow to adult size. *Jeholornis* and *Sapeornis* also took several years to reach adult size. These early birds, along with dinosaurs, had babies before they became full size.

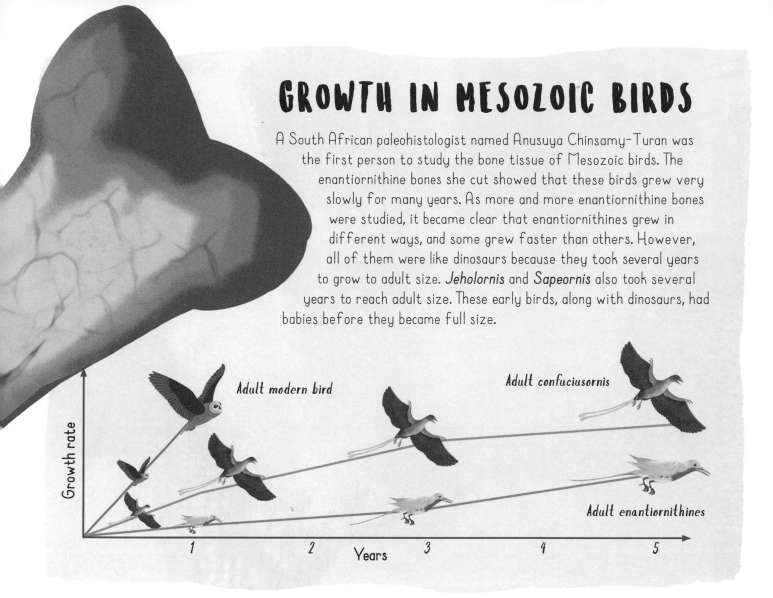

Adult modern bird

Adult confuciusornis

Adult enantiornithines

Growth rate

Years

1   2   3   4   5

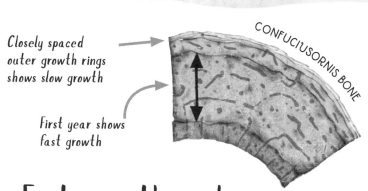

CONFUCIUSORNIS BONE

Closely spaced outer growth rings shows slow growth

First year shows fast growth

Variable growth

In living birds, every adult individual in a particular species is about the same size. However, dinosaurs and early birds were different. Adult *Confuciusornis* have a two-fold size range, which means that some adults are half the size of others. Scientists call this "developmental plasticity." It means that depending on factors like availability of food and other resources, *Confuciusornis* and other basal birds would grow more or grow less.

Fast growth evolves

Growing fast means that a bird spends less time vulnerable and dependent on its parents. The fast type of growth we see in living birds had already evolved in birds by the Early Cretaceous. This type of growth only evolved in the Ornithuromorpha, the group that includes living birds. However, the early pygostylian bird *Confuciusornis* also evolved to grow almost as quickly. Its bone tissue shows us that it grew almost to full size within the first year and then got a tiny bit bigger every year for the next few years, because the growth lines that form the outer portion of its bone are very closely spaced.

Adults grew differently depending on how much food they had

BIRD MUMMIES

There are huge pieces of amber found in the southeast Asian country of Myanmar. Amber is fossilized tree resin—a thick, sticky liquid that oozes out of trees. It's so sticky that animals and plants can get trapped in it! When the resin turns into amber the living things trapped inside become fossils—they are essentially amber mummies. Usually only small animals like insects get trapped in resin, but these chunks of amber are so big that they preserve vertebrates!

Enantiornithine in resin

A long history

The amber from northern Myanmar has been collected for almost 2,000 years. In the past it was used to make jewelry. The Chinese called it "blood amber" because of its unique red color. Myanmar used to be called Burma, and the amber is still known as Burmese amber. The first insects trapped in it were described in 1916. A century later, an amazing discovery was made: two specimens containing the remains of small birds!

Birds in amber

So far at least ten pieces of Burmese amber preserving birds have been found, and two of them represent almost complete birds. All the birds that have been found so far are very small enantiornithines—some are the size of hummingbirds! Some have very strange features that are not found in enantiornithines elsewhere.

Enantiornithine

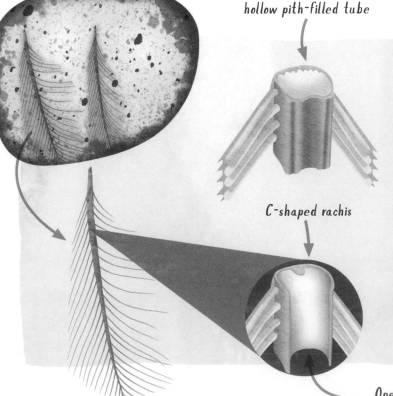

Modern chicken rachis hollow pith-filled tube

C-shaped rachis

Open rachis without pith

STRANGE FEATHERS

Rachis-dominated feathers (see pages 42–43) were first found on birds preserved in rocks. But when the first rachis-dominated feathers were found in amber, they showed that everything we thought we knew about them was wrong! Instead of a modern hollow tube-like rachis, these feathers had one that was C-shaped. It was also very thin—thinner than a piece of paper.

ELEKTORORNIS

Pronounced: ee-LEK-tor-OR-nis
Lived: 99 MYA (Early Cretaceous)
Size: estimated 5 inches long; 10-inch wingspan

The foot of this bird is unlike any other bird, alive or extinct, with a very long middle toe. Paleontologists think that *Elektorornis* used this long toe to probe for grubs in rotting trees. A lemur called an aye-aye does the same thing, except it uses its fingers instead of its toes. Today, birds who feed like this use their beaks and tongue.

FORTIPESAVIS

Pronounced: FOR-ti-pez-AH-vis
Lived: 99 MYA (Early Cretaceous)
Size: estimated 4–5 inches long; 8–10 inch wingspan

All that we know about this little bird comes from an impression of the skin on its foot. The first two of the three forward-facing toes look normal, but the third is unusually wide. The foot may be adapted for perching on branches that move. In modern kingfishers, the second and third toes are connected by skin to form one big outer toe. This increased surface area of the foot helps the bird to get a better grip.

Other cool critters

It's not just birds that have been found in Burmese amber. Paleontologists have found a baby snake, several lizards, a frog, and even a tail that might belong to a baby dinosaur! The first vertebrate found in amber was a gecko, and even the soft tissue of its sticky toepads is preserved. One lizard is so weird that at first scientists thought it was a bird! It turned out to be a lizard that evolved a bird-shaped skull.

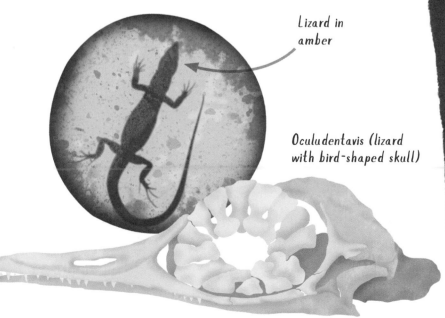

Lizard in amber

Oculudentavis (lizard with bird-shaped skull)

BIRDS OF THE LATE CRETACEOUS

The Late Cretaceous lasted from 100.5–66 MYA. Compared to the Early Cretaceous, there are not many bird fossils known from this time, and most of them are incomplete. Some species have even been named from a single bone—or less! They also don't often preserve soft tissues. This makes it very hard for scientists to understand what these birds were like. What we do know is that primitive bird groups in the Late Cretaceous looked more like living birds in many ways as they evolved to be better at flight.

MIRARCE

Pronounced: meer-AR-key
Lived: 76–74 MYA (Late Cretaceous)
Size: estimated 13 inches long;
45–50 inch wingspan

Mirarce belongs to a group of enantiornithines called the Avisauridae. They were first thought to be non-avian dinosaurs, but they are actually birds. Most avisaurids are known from a single foot bone, but *Mirarce* is known from lots of bones collected in Utah. This bird grew quickly, then slowly, then quickly again, then slowly. *Mirarce* was one of the biggest known enantiornithines.

HESPERORNIS

Pronounced: HESS-per-OR-nis
Lived: 83.5–78 MYA (Late Cretaceous)
Size: up to 6.5 feet long

Hesperornis is the biggest known Cretaceous bird. It had a mouth full of hooked teeth that were adapted for cutting. *Hesperornis* could not fly—in fact, it didn't even have hand bones anymore! It had special feet adapted for swimming, similar to loons and grebes today.

YUORNIS

Pronounced: you-OR-nis
Lived: around 72–66 MYA
(Late Cretaceous)
Size: estimated 11 inches
long; 30–35 inch wingspan

Yuornis, from central China, is the most complete Late Cretaceous enantiornithine that has ever been found. It is preserved in 3D and includes a complete skull. This specimen reveals how enantiornithines and modern birds evolved some of the same skull features, independent of each other. A bone called the postorbital is present in Early Cretaceous enantiornithines but absent in living birds—and also in *Yuornis.* It also has no teeth but the shape of the beak was different from *Gobipteryx.*

GOBIPTERYX

Pronounced: go-BIP-ter-ix
Lived: 75–71 MYA (Late Cretaceous)
Size: estimated 7 inches long;
25-inch wingspan

When *Gobipteryx* was first found in Mongolia, scientists thought it was a relative of the ostrich, but the paleontologist Luis Chiappe later showed that it was an enantiornithine. Like living birds, it had no teeth. Paleontologists have found *Gobipteryx* embryos with well-formed bones preserved in eggs, showing that enantiornithines were super-precocial.

ICHTHYORNIS

Pronounced: ICK-thee-OR-nis
Lived: 95–83.5 MYA (latest Early Cretaceous)
Size: 9 inches long; estimated 30-inch wingspan

Discovered in 1880, the skeleton of *Ichthyornis* looked like that of living birds, except that it had lots of teeth in its jawbones. This, plus its location in marine rocks in Kansas, suggests it ate fish. It flew over the sea and swooped down to catch fish—like gulls do today. The bone at the tip of its snout (the premaxilla) had no teeth, and it probably had a small, hooked beak (that's right, some birds had beaks *and* teeth).

THE RISE OF MODERN BIRDS

Today's birds make up the group Neornithes. This group is incredibly diverse, but this diversity evolved from one ancient common ancestor. The fossil record of modern birds in the Cretaceous is very poor, so there is much we don't understand about the origins of Neornithes. Most specimens are incomplete, and species like *Austinornis* and *Ceramornis* are represented by only a piece of one bone! With so little material to work with, it's no wonder that paleontologists can't decide on what group of birds these specimens belong to.

Cenozoic

66 MYA

Upper Cretaceous

100.5 MYA

Lower Cretaceous

145 MYA

Upper Jurassic
163.5 MYA

Splitting off

The fossils we have tell paleontologists that by the Late Cretaceous, the Neornithes was already splitting. The paleognath group (which today includes ostriches, kiwis, tinamous, emus, cassowaries, and rheas) had split from the neognath group that contained all other birds. In addition, the anseriform group (ducks and geese) and the galliform group (chickens and turkeys) had also split. That means the ancestors of ostriches, ducks, and chickens lived at least 68 MYA.

■ THE STEM

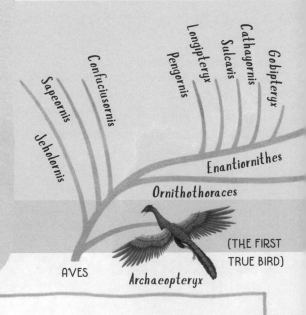

Sapeornis
Confuciusornis
Pengornis
Longipteryx
Sulcavis
Cathayornis
Gobipteryx
Jeholornis
Enantiornithes
Ornithothoraces
AVES
Archaeopteryx
(THE FIRST TRUE BIRD)

The syrinx

VEGAVIS

Pronounced: vay-GAH-vis
Lived: 69-66 MYA (Late Cretaceous)
Size: estimated 10-12 inches; 40-45 inch wingspan

Named after the island in Antarctica where it was found, *Vegavis* was the first good fossil found of a Cretaceous crown bird. It may have been most closely related to ducks. *Vegavis* had several advanced features that are not found in stem birds, such as the syrinx, the avian vocal organ. This is the only Mesozoic fossil syrinx ever found, which may mean that this feature evolved very late and was only present in crown birds.

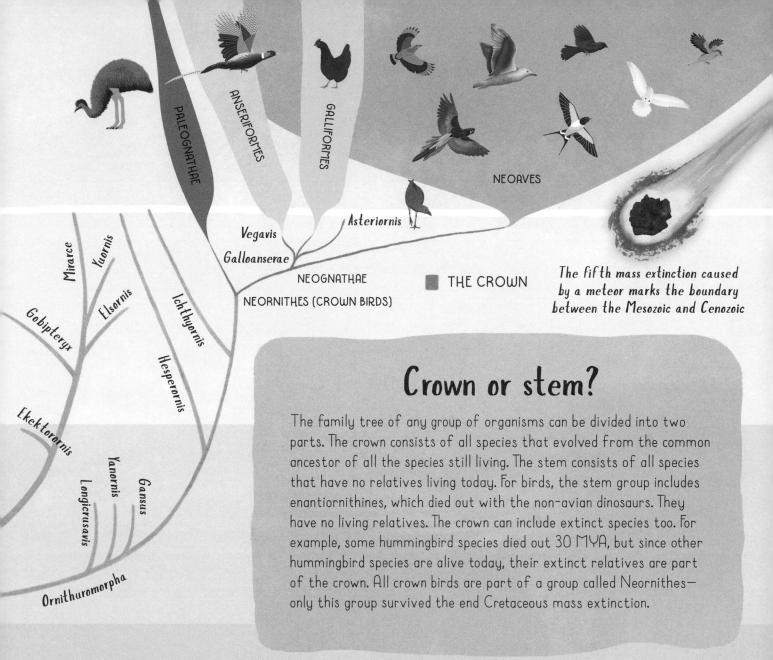

PALEOGNATHAE

ANSERIFORMES

GALLIFORMES

NEOAVES

Mirarce

Yuornis

Elsornis

Gobipteryx

Ichthyornis

Hesperornis

Ekektorornis

Yanornis

Gansus

Longicrusavis

Ornithuromorpha

Vegavis

Galloanserae

Asteriornis

NEOGNATHAE

NEORNITHES (CROWN BIRDS)

■ THE CROWN

The fifth mass extinction caused
by a meteor marks the boundary
between the Mesozoic and Cenozoic

Crown or stem?

The family tree of any group of organisms can be divided into two
parts. The crown consists of all species that evolved from the common
ancestor of all the species still living. The stem consists of all species
that have no relatives living today. For birds, the stem group includes
enantiornithines, which died out with the non-avian dinosaurs. They
have no living relatives. The crown can include extinct species too. For
example, some hummingbird species died out 30 MYA, but since other
hummingbird species are alive today, their extinct relatives are part
of the crown. All crown birds are part of a group called Neornithes—
only this group survived the end Cretaceous mass extinction.

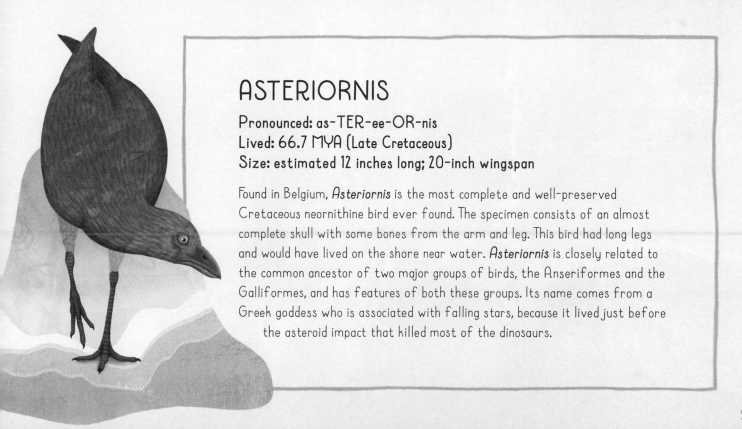

ASTERIORNIS

Pronounced: as-TER-ee-OR-nis
Lived: 66.7 MYA (Late Cretaceous)
Size: estimated 12 inches long; 20-inch wingspan

Found in Belgium, *Asteriornis* is the most complete and well-preserved
Cretaceous neornithine bird ever found. The specimen consists of an almost
complete skull with some bones from the arm and leg. This bird had long legs
and would have lived on the shore near water. *Asteriornis* is closely related to
the common ancestor of two major groups of birds, the Anseriformes and the
Galliformes, and has features of both these groups. Its name comes from a
Greek goddess who is associated with falling stars, because it lived just before
the asteroid impact that killed most of the dinosaurs.

MASS EXTINCTIONS

When at least 75 percent of complex species go extinct in a geologically short period of time, it's called a mass extinction. These events are very clear in the geologic record, with a distinct boundary between rock layers that have plenty of fossils and layers that have hardly any. Mass extinctions always separate two different time intervals. For example, the Permo-Triassic mass extinction, 252 MYA, marked the end of the Paleozoic and the beginning of the Mesozoic.

The Chicxulub impact crater

The fifth mass extinction

There have been five mass extinctions in Earth's history. Around 66 million years ago, all non-avian dinosaurs went extinct, along with pterosaurs, plesiosaurs, mosasaurs, and two major groups of fossil squid. This extinction marked the end of the Cretaceous period and the beginning of the Paleogene, so it is called the End Cretaceous or K-Pg (pronounced pig) mass extinction. It also marks the end of the Mesozoic era and the beginning of the Cenozoic, in which we live.

FINDING CHICXULUB

For a long time no one knew the cause of this mass extinction. The rock layer that marks the boundary has high levels of the element iridium. Iridium is rare on Earth, but common in asteroids. In 1980, the physicist Luis Alvarez proposed that the layer of iridium was caused by a meteor impact. Then, in the 1990s, geologists announced the discovery of a huge crater, 111 miles in diameter, in the Gulf of Mexico. The crater dates from the same time as the K-Pg mass extinction, supporting Dr. Alvarez's idea that it was a meteor that had wiped out the non-avian dinosaurs.

A global disaster

Scientists estimate that the meteor was 6–9 miles wide. When it hit, this released large amounts of sulfur into the atmosphere. Acid rain would have poured down for weeks. The impact also caused a massive tsunami and created a thick cloud of dust that blocked out the sun for months, destroying plant life. But worst of all, scientists think that the ocean surface water became acidic.

OTHER THEORIES

But was the meteor impact the sole cause of the K-Pg mass extinction? Geologists think that some dinosaur lineages, like sauropods, were already in decline. But it's possible that they weren't actually in decline—we just haven't found the fossils yet. Just before the K-Pg boundary, enormous volcanic eruptions began in India, and the gases they spewed out would have caused climate change (this may also have triggered the Permo-Triassic mass extinction). The mass extinction was probably caused by the meteor impact but made worse by these eruptions.

The survivors

Many groups managed to survive beyond the K-Pg boundary, although their numbers were (temporarily) sharply reduced. When life returned to normal levels of diversity, paleontologists were surprised to see which groups had survived. Amphibians were unaffected, even though paleontologists imagine they would be especially vulnerable to things like acidity. While most dinosaurs (including most birds) went extinct, one group survived—Neornithes.

Why did Neornithes survive?

Why did birds like the enantiornithines become extinct while the neornithines survived? This is still a mystery to paleontologists. It may have to do with key differences in neornithine biology, like the fact they grew fast, had chalazae in their eggs, and were better adapted to feed on foods like seeds that could be found during the aftermath of the meteor impact.

THE EVOLUTION OF TODAY'S BIRDS

In the Paleogene the bird family tree rapidly split into the different groups we see today. Scientists call this an explosive radiation because it happened so fast and involved so many new species. The appearance of most major bird groups in just 5–10 million years following the extinction may have been possible because groups like enantiornithines and pterosaurs were now extinct. The meteor essentially eliminated the competition!

TSIDIIYAZHI

Pronounced: TSOO-dee-eye-AH-zee
Lived: 62.5 MYA (Early Paleocene)
Size: estimated 4 inches long;
8-inch wingspan

Tsidiiyazhi was found in New Mexico and has a name from the Navajo language, meaning "little bird." It is a member of a group of birds called mousebirds. Today this group only has six living species and they all live in the Sahara Desert. *Tsidiiyazhi* probably lived in trees, eating fruits and seeds. It could rotate its fourth toe backwards when it wanted, a feature that is good for climbing trees as well as grasping objects like branches.

WAIMANU

Pronounced: why-MON-oo
Lived: 61–58 MYA (Early Paleocene)
Size: 3 feet tall

Waimanu is the oldest known penguin. Its name comes from Maori words meaning "water bird." Fossils of this species are found in New Zealand. Its legs were longer than that of modern penguins, but like them, *Waimanu* stood upright on land and could not fly. However, its wings were adapted for "flying" under water, making it an excellent swimmer. It probably caught fish and squid.

LIMNOFREGATA

Pronounced:
LIM-no-fre-GAH-tuh
Lived: 54–52 MYA
(Eocene)
Size: estimated 20 inches long;
3–4 foot wingspan

Frigatebirds are incredibly agile fliers, harassing other birds in the air and stealing their food. *Limnofregata*, the oldest fossil frigatebird, had a shorter beak that wasn't as hooked as in living frigatebirds, as well as longer legs. *Limnofregata* lived near freshwater lakes in Wyoming, but modern frigatebirds live by the sea.

PULCHRAPOLLIA

Pronounced: PULCH-ruh-
POLE-ee-uh
Lived: 55 MYA (Early Eocene)
Size: estimated 6–8 inches
long; 12–15 inch wingspan

Pulchrapollia was found in the UK. These birds are thought to belong to a group called the Halcyornithidae, which is closely related to parrots. Like living parrots, *Pulchrapollia* had two toes that point forward and two that point backward. Paleontologists think that unlike modern parrots, it may have been carnivorous.

MASILLARAPTOR

Pronounced: muh-SILL-uh-RAP-tor
Lived: 49 MYA (Early to Middle Eocene)
Size: estimated 6–8 inches long;
15–17 inch wingspan

Masillaraptor is thought to be a distant relative of living falcons. It comes from a famous fossil lake in Germany where many species have been described by the paleontologist Gerald Mayr, including this one. It had long legs and a hooked beak that was longer than those of living falcons. Its claws were smaller and not as sharply curved.

EUROTROCHILUS

Pronounced: YOO-roh-troh-KILL-us
Lived: 30 MYA (Oligocene)
Size: estimated 3.5 inches long;
4-inch wingspan

Eurotrochilis looked very much like a living hummingbird, with a long beak and very short wings. Its fossils are found in both Germany and France. This is strange because modern hummingbirds are only found in North and South America. Fossils like these can show how bird distributions have changed over geological time.

THE BIRDS THAT DIDN'T MAKE IT

In the 66 million years since the non-avian dinosaurs became extinct, there have been many different groups of birds that were closely related to the species we see today, but which are no longer alive. And some of them were really cool! These include the largest birds to ever fly and gigantic flightless birds that make ostriches look small.

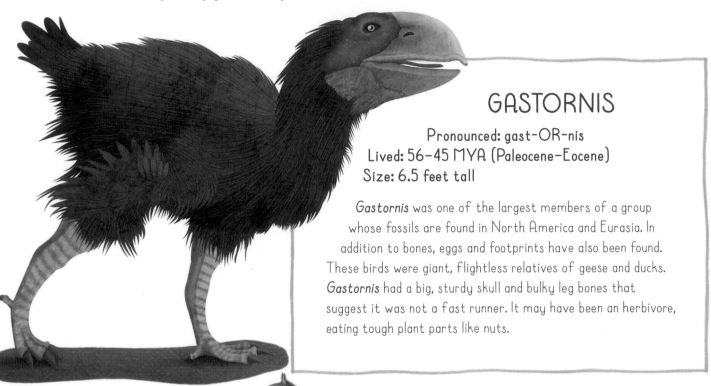

GASTORNIS

Pronounced: gast-OR-nis
Lived: 56–45 MYA (Paleocene-Eocene)
Size: 6.5 feet tall

Gastornis was one of the largest members of a group whose fossils are found in North America and Eurasia. In addition to bones, eggs and footprints have also been found. These birds were giant, flightless relatives of geese and ducks. *Gastornis* had a big, sturdy skull and bulky leg bones that suggest it was not a fast runner. It may have been an herbivore, eating tough plant parts like nuts.

KELENKEN

Pronounced: keh-LEN-ken
Lived: 15 MYA (Miocene)
Size: 10.5 feet tall

Kelenken was a member of a group of predatory flightless birds known as "terror birds" because of their enormous size and carnivorous diet. Terror birds lived from 62–1.8 MYA and were the apex predators in South America during that time. *Kelenken*, which lived in Argentina, was one of the biggest, with a long beak that had a sharp hooked tip. Its leg bones are long and slender, suggesting that it was a fast runner.

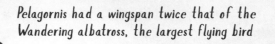

Pelagornis had a wingspan twice that of the Wandering albatross, the largest flying bird

PELAGORNIS

Pronounced: PELL-uh-GORE-nis
Lived: approximately 28–25 MYA (Oligocene)
Size: 5 feet long; 21-foot wingspan

With its huge wingspan, *Pelagornis* was the largest bird ever to fly. Like the other members of its group, it had bony spikes growing off its jaw bones that looked like pointy teeth. These were probably useful for catching slippery fish and squid to eat, similar to the teeth in *Yanornis* and *Ichthyornis*. *Pelagornis* would have soared over the ocean from Antarctica to North America.

VOROMBE

Pronounced: vore-UM-bay
Lived: 2 MYA–1000 CE (Pleistocene-Holocene)
Size: 10 feet tall; weight 1,600 lbs

Vorombe was probably the heaviest bird of all time—it was five times the weight of the heaviest ostrich! *Vorombe* was a species of elephant bird, a group of giant flightless birds that once lived in Madagascar. Now extinct, they were paleognath birds and most closely related to kiwis. Like kiwis, they took several years to reach adult size. Elephant birds had the biggest eggs of any bird—over a foot long with a thick shell. These birds became extinct because of humans destroying their habitat, hunting them, and taking their eggs.

Isolated islands

It's no coincidence that elephant birds lived on an island and became extinct when humans arrived. The same is true of the dodo, which lived on Mauritius. Isolated islands often do not have any large predators, so their birds have not evolved ways to defend themselves. Many island birds lose the ability to fly. These defenseless birds are at risk of extinction through hunting and the introduction of predatorial species brought by people, like rats, cats, and pigs. The kākāpō, a flightless parrot that lives in New Zealand, is currently endangered for this very reason.

Kākāpō

BIRDS TODAY

The birds you see from your window are flying dinosaurs with an evolutionary history that is over 155 million years in the making. Today birds live in every environment, from the cold, icy wastelands of Antarctica to the deserts of Mongolia and Patagonia. They come in all shapes and sizes, ranging from the tiny bee hummingbird to the 320-pound ostrich, with wingspans of up to 12 feet. Birds are very important today, for many reasons.

Rüppell's griffon vulture

Why are birds so diverse?

With at least 10,000 living species, birds are the most diverse group of land-living vertebrates. This is partly because their biology is so advanced that they can survive in almost any environment, including at high elevations with lower amounts of oxygen. The endangered Rüppell's griffon vulture can fly as high as a commercial airplane, where no mammal could survive! In addition, their flexible digestive system allows them to adapt to feed on just about anything.

The many roles of birds

Birds serve important roles in the ecosystems where they live. Birds eat many pests, including caterpillars that in large numbers can kill trees, and rodents which can harm crops and spread disease. Birds are also important in dispersing seeds, and some even act as pollinators. Vultures get rid of carcasses, which helps to stop the spread of disease.

Birds and humans

Birds are an important part of our lives. In ancient times, people even worshipped them! To the ancient Egyptians, the ibis was the symbol of the god Thoth, while an owl was the symbol of Athena, the Greek goddess of wisdom. In North America, totem poles are carved with thunderbirds, a supernatural creature of power. In China, images of an immortal phoenix have been found in artifacts 8,000 years old. Eagles have been used as symbols of empires and countries for over a thousand years, from the Romans to the United States.

Feathers in our lives

If you live somewhere cold, odds are that you use feathers in your everyday life. Feathers fill our down comforters and warm jackets. Feathers have also been used in weapons, to help arrows fly straight. They are used by fishermen as lures. And many different cultures, at many different times, have used feathers for fashion. Ancient Egyptians wore feathers in honor of Ma'at, the goddess of truth. Indigenous North Americans made feathers into elaborate headdresses, sometimes called war bonnets. In the Middle Ages, knights in Europe wore feathers on their helmets and in Venice, feathers adorned the masks worn during Carnival. They are still worn during Carnival in Brazil, a tradition brought by Portuguese settlers.

Dinosaurs on the menu

Throughout our entire history, humans have been eating birds and their eggs. In fact, our Neanderthal relatives probably did too. At first, birds were a fairly minor food source, because they are hard to catch and don't have a lot of meat. The chicken was domesticated in northeastern China as early as 5000 BCE but this was for sport, not food. Ancient Egyptians may have been the first people to domesticate birds for food. They also developed a system of artificial incubation so that their birds could produce more eggs. If a hen doesn't have to sit on its egg, it will keep laying more.

THE SIXTH MASS EXTINCTION

New species are always evolving, while old species go extinct—this is called background extinction. Today, species are going extinct at a rate of at least 100 times the normal rate—possibly as much as 1,000 times! This is much too high to be considered normal background extinction. About three species go extinct every hour, so how many species became extinct while you read this book? Scientists think that we are living through the Earth's sixth mass extinction, and this time, it wasn't caused by a meteor. It's humans that are to blame.

An unusual cause

No previous mass extinction was caused by an animal, but it is overwhelmingly clear that humans are the cause of the sixth mass extinction. Our over-consumption leads to the destruction of habitats. We pollute the environment and cause climate change, which in turn acidifies the ocean. Our actions have driven many species to extinction and over 40,000 more are currently endangered.

KNOWLEDGE AND COMPASSION

Knowing about the problem is not enough. The facts show that human actions are harming animals and poisoning our environment, yet still we do not change. We need more than knowledge—we need compassion to guide our actions. Compassion is concern for the suffering of others, including the animals we depend on.

A CONNECTED WORLD

Scientists think that if we do not stop driving living species to extinction, we too will go extinct. No species can survive alone—each is part of a complex ecosystem that includes many other species. Organisms interact with each other in many ways, relying on each other for more than just food. Plants and algae provide us with the oxygen we breathe, and there are thousands of species of bacteria living in our stomachs and on our skin, without which we cannot survive.

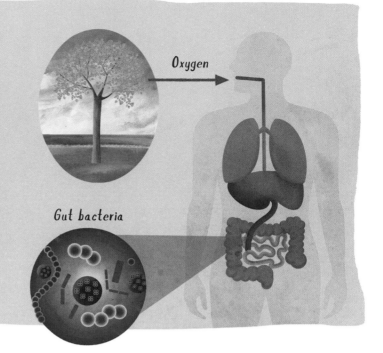

Oxygen

Gut bacteria

How are birds affected?

Humans were the cause of the extinction of the dodo and the elephant bird. More recently, the passenger pigeon went extinct in 1914 due to overhunting and habitat loss. We also harm birds with the chemicals we use. The pesticide DDT reduced the populations of many birds by thinning their eggshells, so the babies died before hatching. Although now banned in many countries, birds are still dying because traces of DDT remain in the environment.

Wanting too much

The problem is over-consumption. Today most of our desires are created by companies that target the unconscious part of the brain to make us want things we don't necessarily need. They even make us feel bad if we don't have them. Over-consumption means that we are using up so many resources (such as water, fish, and trees) that it is causing ecosystems to collapse. Most species are adapted to live in specific habitats. When humans destroy these habitats, these species go extinct.

WHAT WE CAN DO

If we are the cause, we can also be the solution! As the Chinese thinker Confucius once said, "Improve yourself and there will be peace under the sky." This means to change the world all we need to do is change ourselves. By thinking about how our actions affect the planet, we can make decisions that consider its long-term health. What is good for the planet is good for us—and it's good for birds and other animals too.

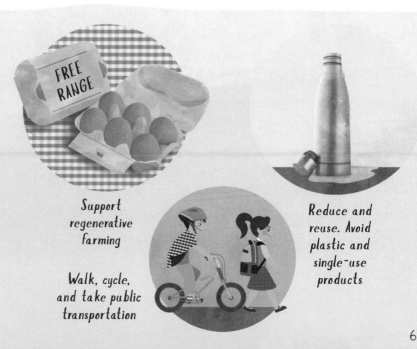

FREE RANGE

Support regenerative farming

Walk, cycle, and take public transportation

Reduce and reuse. Avoid plastic and single-use products

INDEX